COINCIDENCE OR MIRACLE

COINCIDENCE OR MIRACLE

BY:
PETER ANTHONY MOORE

XULON PRESS

Xulon Press
2301 Lucien Way #415
Maitland, FL 32751
407.339.4217
www.xulonpress.com

Xulon PRESS

Unless otherwise indicated, Scripture quotations taken from the King James Version (KJV) – *public domain.*

Paperback ISBN-13: 978-1-6628-4215-3
Ebook ISBN-13: 978-1-6628-4216-0

Dedications

Iris

Iris Lee's poetry book Urban Bird Life was published by NYQ Books in 2010. She's a native Brooklynite. She co-leads a writing workshop for theater professionals at the Actors Fund and studies at the Writers Studio in The Village. Her website is irisleepoet.com

I joined The, with a capital T, Actors writing workshop in 200? after being hospitalized. Iris led me through a writing process that healed me. Most importantly, there was always this look in her eye that said, "Peter, you could do it."

Julia Cameron

I had a dream of opening a healing center in Coney Island Brooklyn's Royal Bath House. There it was, all locked up and hidden behind the train station—a royal palace, closed down and begging the universe to use me. I joined Community Board 13. I met all there were to meet. I got phone numbers from the front gate. I called the right people. There it was, a beautiful, royal castle closed up in a community that could really benefit from an awesome healing center in Coney Island Brooklyn. The whole journey led me to the healing mecca in Manhattan. I got there, only to find that Julia Cameron was going to be there that day doing a seminar. I wasn't signed up. So, I couldn't attend. I stuck my head in the room as her classroom participants entered. She came into the room like the fairy godmother in The Wizard of Oz. She looked over at me and winced. I kissed her back telepathically. Her book The Artist's Way birthed the writer in me. I am forever grateful.

Terry McFadden

While attending church service at Faithful Central (Bishop Kenneth Ulmer) in Inglewood, California, Terry McFadden ministered and called all writers out from the congregation. She invited me to a writer's meet-up. I took a leap of faith and went to the meeting. When I got there, the room was filled with all kinds of experienced writers; I was so honored. 9/11 had just happened. Our prompt was to create a character from the disaster. The whole room was amazed by what I created. The whole room unanimously agreed that not only was I a good writer, but they all could tell by the way that I write that I am a native New Yorker. Thank you, Terry McFadden. Ain't no stopping us now!

Foreword

───◆───

This is for the broken-hearted, stifled, diligent and loyal, prudent, everything-right folk who didn't get paid. So-smart-that-nothing's-funny folk. Sexually repressed, church abused, bamboozled, walking dead. Too sweet, too beautiful, genuine, politically abused, proud, heady, tired-of-being-shut-up-and-cheated-on folk who can't find joy. The sour, bitter, everything's-too-late people. Yea but heads, drag queens, pimps, nuns, oppressed leaders, good working moms, organization-repressed social misfits, boxheads who need to laugh, royal families, the homeless, spent, too girly, too manly, unidentifiable-closet-criers-who-have-been-squarely-treated-unfairly-and-nothing-really-matters folks, and anyone else who would dare to open their minds to the supernatural.

Intro

I would like for you to open your heart and spirit. Love is the message that this book speaks to you personally. I reference Jesus and the King James Bible for most of this book. This is how revelation and enlightenment came to me. Whatever metaphysical engagement you use, if any, is fine. I'm referring to past lives, angels, higher selves, notions of karmic debt, etc. However you get to that divine enlightenment is your unique journey. I have personally had many experiences that are beyond ordinary explanations. This has made me non-judgmental and open-minded. It is not the reality or validity of these various supernatural entities that is the issue. I'm asking that you open your mind to the base root of humanity in this journey and extrapolate the messages for the betterment of your present-day circumstances.

You will be tickled and laugh with joy as you take this ride of mere ridicules.

Be aware of "Vuyo's But Theory."

You Laughing!

He he hell,
Smoking fire smells,
And I still strugg to strugg gelle.
42nd Street's no more,
Full of male and female whores,
Shops of porn, just takes a glance.
Sneaky peeps left up to chance.
Boobs and booths to overlook.
Raging twenties, hormonally hooked.
Instinctually knowing the good, good book.
Sex, no rings.
Bells, dingalings.
Church steals, mental intercept games.
Humble and broken, dumbfounded and ousted.
Hippies and models and singers and spouses.
Control freaks, fanatics, worldly and shrewd, International
and funny,
A real motley crew.
Dynamic in stewing, hand-picked for sure.
In your face for realness.
You know that you know.
Testimony can't steal
Mere ridicules of stance
The truth reveals.
Ridiculous significance,
A riddle to many.
The mouth will seal.
Still think it's funny?
Justice not will,
Farrakhan said it nice.

And love from Islam with a bean pie slice.
Psalm 37 says fret not thyself.
Grandma's from heaven is the true wealth.
Naturally super, lean not to your mind,
Finite, in its make-up.
Okay, how do you find
The answers lit, to how and to why?
Open and trust,
It waits for you. Sigh.

Today I was happy right now because it seemed as if I was about to embark on a great new job. Then I started to doubt myself. I thought, I hope this isn't a trap or a set-up. So, I looked at my phone. When I looked at the messages, the name of my new job was on the phone. I thought, That's strange. I opened the whole message. On a previous message, my friend had asked me, "What time should we meet?" I had texted her back, "5:30," which happens to be the name of the new company that I will be working for. It's just the little things sometimes that you' d like to call

Coincidence:
A situation in which events happen at the same time in a way that is not planned or expected.
- The occurrence of two or more things at the same time
- The state of two or more things being the same

Miracle
An extraordinary event manifesting divine intervention in human affairs.
- An extremely outstanding or unusual event, thing, or accomplishment

- Christian science: a divinely natural phenomenon experienced humanly as the fulfillment of spiritual law

The difference between coincidences and miracles is that miracles manifest divine intervention and fulfill spiritual law.

Take a chance.

Step Out in Faith

46 And they came to Jericho: and as he went out of Jericho with his disciples and a great number of people, blind Bartimaeus, the son of Timaeus, sat by the highway side begging.

47 And when he heard that it was Jesus of Nazareth, he began to cry out, and say, Jesus, thou Son of David, have mercy on me.

48 And many charged him that he should hold his peace: but he cried the more a great deal, Thou Son of David, have mercy on me.

49 And Jesus stood still, and commanded him to be called. And they call the blind man, saying unto him, Be of good comfort, rise; he calleth thee.

50 And he, casting away his garment, rose, and came to Jesus.

51 And Jesus answered and said unto him, What wilt thou that I should do unto thee? The blind man said unto him, Lord, that I might receive my sight.

52 And Jesus said unto him, Go thy way; thy faith hath made thee whole. And immediately he received his sight, and followed Jesus in the way.

Sometimes you might have to cry out to receive your miracle. This blind man Bartimaeus cried out, and God rewarded him with a miracle

Don't let anyone talk you out of your miracle.
Bartimaeus's new testimony was,

Once I was blind;
But now I see.

Don't let anyone steal your testimony.

Hey, that rhymes! Once I was blind, but now I see. No teef my testimony. Jah rule!

You know that that blind man couldn't care less about any of the ridicules that were coming his way because now he was hearing them with open eyes, literally. They could ridicule and laugh as hard as they wanted, but the hard facts were too real for him to pay them any mind. My prayer is that after you finish reading this book, you will experience some hard facts, miracles that change the rest of your life journey forever...

Know that you know that you know.

"Golden abundance" -Peter Anthony Moore's artwork

Mere Ridicules

Table of Contents

How Do You Know?

———◆———

N ow you tell me. Would you consider this a coincidence or a miracle? This was the first time that I knew the difference.

My girlfriend and I were preparing to marry. We made our wedding plans and were all set to go. My prayer was, "Jesus, please let me know if there is any reason why I shouldn't marry this girl. In Jesus's name I pray, Amen." I knew how much she loved her male friends. So, they had to know that she was now getting married. We discussed it. I asked her to let me know if she needed to clear things with them. I loved sleeping with her at her apartment. We went to bed peacefully that night. When I woke up, I asked her, "Hey boo, what about your first love?" Her eyes bulged out of her head.

"Peter, Peter, why are you asking me that?" She was flustered.

I said, "Well I know that first love is a strong thing. Are you still in love with him?"

"No, no," she replied. See, but I had to look at his picture on her dresser every time I came over. Hmm...suspect.

"Are you sure you're not still in love with him?"

"No, no, please, my mother would kill me. No, no, but why are you asking me that?"

"Just asking."

Sunday morning came. I was sitting in church (St. Paul's Baptist, East New York Brooklyn). The service started. I didn't see my girlfriend. That's strange. She'd usually be here by now. I kept turning around and looking all around the sanctuary trying to find her. Finally, I spotted her. She was sitting way in the back. I mouthed to her, "Why are you sitting there? I saved a seat for you." She waved her hand at me, "It's okay, I'll tell you after service." When the church service finished, I walked over to her. "Hey, why didn't you come and sit with me?" She gave me a story. Okay. Well, that day was a big day for me. I was going to see a play that I was being considered for. Mr. Cosby was involved. I told my girlfriend as I prepared to get home. She asked me why I was acting so strange. I said, "Me, acting strange? You're the one who came to church and didn't sit with me. Anyways, I'll call you after my audition."

So, I went home and prepared for my audition. I took the E train to West 4th Street. When I stepped out of the train, I looked up, and my girlfriend was being escorted by a very happy guy. It just so happened that they were on the same train that I was on and riding the car in front of me. I froze. The two of them were so elated to see each other. Exiting the station, the guy walked through the turnstiles and opened his sheepskin coat. He said, "Yeah, look at my baby!" with a big smile. She came through the turnstiles and fell into his arms. I lost my heart at that moment. I was slowly approaching the guy, and we caught eyes. OMG, it was the guy on her dresser! My girlfriend was laughing and giggling in pure joy. She fell in his arms, and he said, "I'm home, baby. I'm so happy to see you!" I walked slowly behind them. When I came out of the station, they were at the corner, hugging and cuddling on their way toward 8th Street. I looked at the garbage can. I thought, If I approached them, and he came to attack me, I would have to bust a bottle over his head. The garbage cans had some bottles in it. I'm going to have to bust his head open. He just got out of jail. This is going to be bloody. Don't do it. Go to your audition. I followed them and saw them go inside BBQ's on 8th Street and sit down at a window. They sat so excited to see one another. I watched them for a while, and then I headed out to my audition.

The next day, my girlfriend called me, "Hey." She proceeded to tell me about her night out with her girlfriend. She mentioned a movie that she had already seen.

I tried to interject, "You saw that movie already."

She replied, "Oh, my girlfriend didn't, so I decided to watch it again." She continued on with her story. I tried to interject; she kept on talking.

I couldn't get a word in, and then I yelled out, "Stop! Stop! Stop! I saw you last night."

She stopped rambling. "What?"

"I saw you last night."

"Oh my God, Peter, you know I was thinking that as I was going into the restaurant. What would Peter think if he saw me right now? Or if someone else saw me who would go back and tell you. Peter, it is not what you think." She started to cry. "I was telling him about you. Please, Peter, let's talk this over."

I had asked her to tell me if she had to deal with any of her current male friends—let them know that she would be getting married soon and that things were going to change. "If you have to get together with them to let them know about your upcoming marriage, please let me know." Soooooo...she didn't do that. But bigger than that, she lied about the night that she had out. When I tried to stop her, she kept on going on, fabricating this night out with her girlfriend. That is why I decided to not marry her. I couldn't believe how she could lie to me so easily. When I saw her that night, her face was glowing. She was so happy to see her first love out of jail. So, if she's lying to me like that now, how much more later on? I called off our wedding.

Was this mere coincidence or a miracle?

Divine intervention makes it a miracle.

I know it was a miracle because it was the first time that I had ever prayed like that. I prayed and asked God to reveal to me any reason why I shouldn't marry this girl. God answered by somehow having us on the same train, getting off at the same stop, one car behind the other. Amazingly, I was in the car behind them and not them behind me.

The truth was revealed.

It was also a personal revelation.

Noun, | rev*e*la*tion | ˌre-və-ˈlā-shən

Definition of revelation
:an act of revealing or communicating divine truth
:something that is revealed by God to humans
:an act of revealing to view or making known
:something that is revealed
:an enlightening or astonishing disclosure shocking revelations
:a pleasant often enlightening surprise her talent was a revelation

What a revelation.

God, Source, That answers prayers.

Get in the Water

"Wisdom Waves" Peter Anthony Moore's artwork

Jolly Rogers

I was thirteen.

You know how somehow there's this irks in your mind when you see the ad or commercial for something. It looks real good on the poster, but in reality, it's not all that. Whenever any family member went to Barbados, they always brought me back a Jolly

Roger's T-shirt. I couldn't wait to ride the Jolly Roger's ship. I heard stories from the adults in my family of good party times. The T-shirts said it all.

So, the day had finally come. Yay, I was boarding the Jolly Roger's. It was a perfect Barbados day; I could hear the sweet sounds of Mr. Magic (https://youtu.be/UbsbqkgzxWM). It was hot, and the smell and the breeze from the waters were intoxicating. The ship was kind of old and rickety, but I had love all around. As soon as I got on, I made sure and checked out all of the special parts of the ship. We finally pulled off. Barbados Wharf became smaller and smaller. We finally were out in the deep blue seas. Now on the T-shirt, it shows a big giant swordfish jumping out of the water. Yeah, right. In a split second, just as I thought it, one jumped out of the water directly across from where I was sitting on the boat! I was so fascinated. The whole boat went, "Awww! It was as if the fish and I caught eyes; And then it splashed back in the water. The experience for me was way better than the T-shirt iron-on. When the giant swordfish went back down in the water, I looked up, and a sweet old lady looked me directly in my face and said, "That was just for you." I sat in awe for a minute. Then my favorite song "Magga dog" came on, so I caught up with my family to join in the dance.

I believe that we receive and can enjoy these kinds of life rewards better when we come into them with childlike faith. Then straightway after the phenomena, we move on with a knowing and join right back in the dance of life.

Avenue H

H as in, how, how, how, do these things happen? Easter was always my favorite time of the year. I always knew without a shadow of a doubt that I was going to have one of the best outfits on the block. When Easter came, all of my cousins would be coming to visit, and we would be going to show off our new clothes. Easter for me as a child was about having the best outfit. One Easter, I threw a fit with my mother because she didn't get me the shoes that completed my outfit. I wanted to have the marshmallow shoes like all of my older cousins. I was furious. I was going to be laughed at. How was I going to look in my new studded jean outfit without the shoes to match? Plus, I had showed my mother the shoes that I wanted when we went down to Pitkins Avenue shopping. I had seen them in the window of Buster Brown's. Buster Brown's was the only store that had marsh-mallow shoes for kids. The other stores didn't have marshmallow shoes in my size. My Easter was ruined. Finally, my godfather

Bobby Estavan came through for me and got me my first pair of marshmallow shoes from Buster Brown's on Pitkins Avenue. Now we're talking! Now my Easter was complete. This is what Easter was all about for me.

Yes, yes, yes. When Easter came, my grandmother was not only going to cook, but she was going to bake. And yes, all of my cousins were going to come over, and we were going to play and compare afros. This particular Easter was the best because I had gotten my marshmallow shoes from Buster Brown's, and I was going to be dressed like the big boys.

Oh yeah, we went to church. We went to church and fell asleep in the pews in our brand-new outfits. We couldn't wait for church to be over so that we could come home and eat and then go outside and play with our friends on the block and show off our new outfits. This was Easter.

My great-grandmother would sit in the window and scream down at us while we played outside. I ignored her on that day. Children and their cousins from everywhere were on our block this day. It was too loud.

"What? What? Mama, I can't hear you. What?"

"You hear me, boy, stop running over!"

"What, what, I can't hear you!"

My great-grandmother was mean as hell. I was not one of her favorites in the family. My sister was her favorite. The only way for me to get some sweet time in with her was when she would ask me to come into her room and powder under her breasts and read the Bible for her. I was a very good reader at a young age. I got the chance to sit where she sat and look out of that window, only if I was reading that Bible to her. I knew that it would be all good and I could sit by her window only if I picked up that Bible and began to read. This was my real introduction to the Bible. When my great-grandmother Ersula Ifill died and my family moved from East New York Brooklyn to Laurelton, Queens, that ended church.

My first girlfriend, Patricia Milanes, in Laurelton lived a couple of doors over. She was involved in all kinds of fun things, dance music and playing house, LOL. She went to a Catholic church where all of these things were going on. One day, I woke up and decided to go to this church. Some of my other friends from school were there and, most importantly, Patricia was there. Me and my new best friend Micheal Milanes, Patricia's brother, became altar boys. That didn't last too long because Father David had an unusual accent, and he always chewed the bread of life really funny. Michael and I could not resist the laughter during communion. So, one day, Father David couldn't take it anymore, and he threw Michael and me off of the pulpit and made us sit in the front row of the pews. That was even more distracting for him because now he could see us giggling and cracking up at his accent and the way he chewed the bread. We just didn't fit in.

But I began to love those people outside of my immediate family. I liked it. As a matter of fact, although I don't really see those people anymore, there is still such a burning love in my heart for those people. I found extended family (the church).

Performing Arts

When I got into high school, I wanted to get into some after-school activities. It seemed as if this is where all the fun and creativity started. One of the students decided that she wanted to start some singing in the school. She had a strong church background. She started the school's first gospel choir. I joined to be involved in something other than the mandated curriculum. This was my introduction to the black church. We practiced after school at Harlequin Studios in Manhattan, and we prayed together. The prayers had rhythm and structure. After those prayers went up, everyone would get emotional, and then some would go into an out of control fit, falling all over the place and babbling in between hallelujahs. This was the way the black church got to their divine enlightenment. I came to love the singing. But when everyone started going into the fit and falling out babbling, I wasn't there. I wasn't that emotional about it.

We began to visit local churches. I noticed that when we sang well, it stirred up everyone's emotions, and then they too fell out babbling in between hallelujahs.

I began to feel left out. I wanted to come to this higher place of spiritual bliss. Our high school choir became the first gospel choir from the 120 West 46th St High School of Performing Arts. Not only did we become the school's first gospel choir, we also won the best high school gospel competition and beat out our annex school Music and Art. That day was outrageous. We had to skip school to compete. We all took a chance, and it paid off. I still didn't have the emotional fit of bliss, falling out helpless and babbling in between hallelujahs experience. But, I began to realize that something unexplainable was tugging at me.

Years later, while rehearsing for a Broadway-bound play called Down to Earth, one of the cast members, Art Palmer, kept stirring conversations about marriage and faith and spirituality and church. After talking with me for a while, he said, "You know what?"

"What?"

"You should join this church here in New York that would be great for you."

Gregory Burge was the star of our play, and both Art and I were understudying his part. I really admired Gregg Burge and would be honored to go to the church that he attended. So, Art and I decided to visit one Sunday.

Ooh wee, this was definitely a new experience. The first thing I noticed was a hippie in tight shredded jeans singing next to a girl who was singing in sign language, but she could speak… umm…okay. The atmosphere was very different. It seemed as if the whole cast of the Broadway show Dreamgirls attended this church. The speaker looked like Santa Claus. He spoke like a black preacher. He was explosive and full of life. The congregation received him well, and everyone had the falling out fit, babbling in between hallelujahs experience.

This would be a new experience for me. So, I decided to join this church. I came back the next Sunday, and the great evangelist who had spoken when I joined the church was not there. He was not the pastor of this church. The church was pastored by a very small in stature but large in spirit black woman (Pastor Maria D Lites). She looked like the beautiful dolls that most West Indian and Spanish people have adorning their homes. She was sweet, yet she was extremely powerful. She gave an altar call after she had finished preaching. Here was my chance; maybe I might get that feeling like everybody else got. So, I answered the call. When I stood before her, she asked me to lift my hands up. It was a sign of surrender. I was open. So, I closed my eyes and lifted my hands. I felt like a kite. My arms felt as if they were being billowed open by a rushing wind. When I opened my eyes, I was laying on my back. OMG, no way. I didn't feel it when I fell. I looked up at her in shock. She looked down at me and called for assistance. The elders of the church came over to me to pick me up. She looked me in my face and said, "He is getting emotional." I was in shock. I couldn't believe that I was on the ground. My church experience had just leaped to the next level. I was finally overwhelmed by something that my mind couldn't explain.

Okay, okay, so I made a decision. I then decided to become a member of this church. Down to Earth, the play that I was in, came to an end. The Firestone family couldn't afford to fund their vision of the whole cast up and flying away at the end. No New York Theater at the time could do this. I was offered a dancing part on Coming to America, and my buddy Art Palmer hooked me up with Paula Abdul and Aurora but, I turned it down, being faithful to the project that I was already in...aaaaaaargh, hate that.

So, now my buddy Art Palmer went back to his home in Los Angeles, and I was left in a new church experience by myself. As my time continued with this church (Unbroken Chain), the pastor began to constantly speak negatively about show business and the people in it. She kept saying that the whole industry was of the devil. She began to prophesy over performers to leave their professions. It was so strange because most of the congregation were performing artists. Gregg Burge left the church, and so did most of the performing artists and cast of Dreamgirls. A major exodus happened. I stayed put because I had experienced some-thing that I had never experienced before.

The church was located in Hell's Kitchen on 41st Street and 9th Avenue (Carroll Studios). A little guy named Jimmy made it possible for service to happen in a music studio. It brought him some constant money, other than music rentals. It was conve-nient for me. My new job, now that I too had left show business, SMH, was 1040 on 40th and 6th Avenue.

The church was on 41st between 8th and 9th Avenues at the back of the Port Authority bus station. The church was next door to an underground sleazy bar. It was where the buses parked at Port Authority and exited onto the freeway. The sidewalk was slick with oil, and the air was full of gas fumes. But when we got inside that little studio, we turned it into our oasis in the midst of chaos.

It was perfect for me because I didn't have far to go once I finished work. I'd run over to church for Bible study on Mondays, Wednesday midweek service, Friday night prayer, Saturday dance ministry, and Sunday church, and back to work on Monday. What a schedule. I loved my new church. We became a close-knit family. I was in the helps ministry. I cleaned the bathrooms before service, swept up, and organized the chairs. On Sundays, we had extra rooms to prepare for the children's ministries. I loved helping my pastor. She was such a sweet woman of God. She didn't play any games though. If she saw something, she'd call it out. She was a powerful seer. We were faithful to her. I learned to follow Jesus and really believe in God through her. She told me that most people think that when you give your life to Jesus, your life is going to get boring. She let me know not so. Your life is going to be more exciting than ever. I thought to myself, Yeah right, Pastor. Don't worry, I believe.

So now years later, I was good and settled in this church. I had a great new motley crew of friends. But it seemed as if familiarity had begun to get in the way. It seemed like whatever I talked to my elder about, he got up and spoke about it whenever he got up to minister. No way; I hated this. I started to feel funny talking around him. I told him about my sticky situation with my buddy that I was living with in Harlem. It was not good at all. I found myself in a situation where I had to get out of his apartment like yesterday. So, when the elder of the church (CB) got up to bring the message that Wednesday, he kept interjecting elements that were too close to what he and I had spoken about privately. I was so irritated. This was not the Holy Spirit speaking through him. This was the elder taking from our conversation and building his message. I was not trying to hear him. He went on about the Lord answering our prayers and we, the congregation, not receiving because we don't see it as coming from God. God is giving us the answer, but we refuse because of the way that the answer is coming to us. No, no, I wasn't hearing it. He mentioned that the drummer in the church was looking for a roommate and that there were people sitting

13

here in the church who needed a place to stay, but they wouldn't receive their blessings. I wasn't trying to hear that. He was only saying that because of our previous conversation. So, finally, service ended. As we were exiting, I kept thinking about what had been said over the pulpit. Nah, no way. The drummer who he spoke of who needed a roommate and his friends were going to a nearby diner. They invited me along. I was resistant. Finally, they asked me, "Why don't you take a look at the drummer's apartment? You might like it." Maybe, I thought, but the drummer was too weird for me. I just couldn't imagine us living together. But I took a breath and took a chance. I rode with the drummer (Chris Allen) to his apartment. When we got off of the train, it was in a dark alley. We walked right to the corner and right inside of the building. When he showed me the apartment, I was more than surprised. It looked like a huge dance studio, with big mirrors and a grand piano. Wow. I couldn't tell much about the neighborhood by looking out of the windows. It was a dark night. The drummer suggested that I spend the night and then go check out the neighborhood in the morning while he was at work. He gave me the keys.

So, I went along. That morning when I woke up, I couldn't believe how beautiful the neighborhood was. I couldn't see it at night. The apartment building that I was in was the only apartment building in that area. The neighborhood was adorned with humongous houses with great lawns and huge trees lining the sidewalks. This neighborhood was amazingly beautiful. I walked up my block to get to the main road. When I got to the main road, I absolutely lost it. No way. I ran over to the corner to see if it was really true, and yes, it was true.

It was the dentist office that my mother used to bring us to when I was a child. I ran inside the office. I was so excited, I had tears of joy. I couldn't believe it. I asked for the dentist. They told me that he was gone. I ran out and sat in the exact spot that I had sat in fifteen years ago, when I had told my mother that I loved this neighborhood and that I wished I could live here. What?! Yes, yes, yes.

There it was—the train station across the street from the dentist on Foster Avenue, where they always had clowns and cotton candy. The houses were so big that some people had horses in their yards. I had said to my mother years ago, "Mummy, I like where we live, but could we live over here?"

My mother answered me and said, "Peter, we can't live over here because they only let Jewish people live over here."

Wow, fifteen years later, there I was sitting in the same spot that I had sat in when I was five years old asking my mother if we could move to this neighborhood, with keys in my hand to my now-affirmed new apartment with my new roommate, who happened to be of Jewish descent. Wow, what a coincidence? I think not.

When I had asked my mother if I could live here when I was five, God, Source, That answered when I became an adult. Might not answer when you want it, but miracles are right on time. God heard my prayer when I was a child.

3Blessed [be] the God and Father of our Lord Jesus Christ, who hath blessed us with all spiritual blessings in heavenly [places] in Christ: 4According as he hath chosen us in him before the foundation of the world, that we should be holy and without blame before him in love: 5Having predestinated us unto the adoption of children by Jesus Christ to himself, according to the good pleasure of his will, Hello!

Opened Vision

"Opened vision"

Joining the church was good. It was, for lack of a better phrase, a good eye-opener. But, I still wasn't quite awakened to the out-right mind-blowing phenomena. I didn't know that something so beyond my finite mind was stirring. Somewhere in my gut, I knew that it was all good. Something real good was cooking. In reflection, I thought back to the day that my natural eyes were opened in an opened-eyed night vision while I was awake and seeking divine guidance.

I was coming home from a late-night service at the Unbroken Chain Church. I was riding home on the D train. I noticed these three church ladies examining me. I had just come out of church service, so I was all prayed up. When I got off at Avenue H, they got off with me and then started questioning what church I belonged to. Oh, but then they started verbally bashing my pastor and tried to persuade me that the pastor and the church that I was attending was wrong (because she was a woman) and that I'd better get out of it, or else.

"Can we pray for you, young man?" Well, I knew how to pray. My pastor had told me to plead the blood because those devils can't stand the blood of Jesus. So, we grabbed hands and made a circle in the middle of the dead-end street, and we began to pray. As they were praying, wo was I...out loud! "Lord Jesus, I thank you for Your blood right now in the name of Jesus." And they prayed, and I prayed, and that was that.

We departed, and I turned the corner and went into my apartment building. The whole situation was kind of disturbing to me. I was affected by the way they spoke of my pastor and my church. I fell on my knees in the middle of my apartment. I looked up into the heavens, and it was like an infusion of smoke filtered in and made the Romans symbols 11, and then T smoked in, and then I, then M, then 3, semicolon 14. It said II Timothy 3:14. I looked into the air at this vision and thought, "Wow, I really have a great imagination." There is probably not even a scripture like this in the Bible. So, like the Bereans, I tried to find it in my Bible. I was shocked that, yes, it was a scripture. There was actually a scripture II Timothy 3:14. But what was even more astonishing was what it said. There was a personal spiritual emphasis on the "but." Whenever God starts talking with a "but," it is time to stop and pay close attention. The scripture in front of my eyes read, "But as for you continue in the things in which you have learned and have been assured of know in whom thou hast learned them."

In other words, stay at your church, and your pastor is just fine. What a miracle moment.

Whenever God uses "but," it is time to stop and pay close attention. "But" is used 3,819 times in the Bible.

While reading this book, I would like you to pause and reflect on "Vuyo's but theory" whenever you see
"but."

Vuyo's But Theory

But God changed His mind.
Law killeth but the Spirit giveth life.
But I am a Sovern God.
But our ways are not His ways.
But you survived.

Whenever you see the but,
Just know
That despite all of our shortcomings, miracles will still happen.

conjunction
on the contrary; yet:
I could have died, but I recovered.

except; save:
She was so overjoyed, she could do nothing but weep.

unless; if not; except that (followed by a clause, often with that expressed):
Nothing would do but that I should come in.
  4. without the circumstance that:
    It never rains, but it pours.

5. otherwise than:
   There is no hope but by prayer.
6. that (used especially after doubt, deny, etc. with a
   negative):
   I do doubt, but He will do it.

You could have spent your time reading someone else's book, but you decided to read this book. While reading it, you received divine revelation that was so personal to you that the interaction let you know that there is.

Don't let anyone talk you out of your miracle.

II Timothy 3:14
14 But continue thou in the things which thou hast learned and hast been assured of, knowing of whom thou hast learned them;

A Divine Interception

It was a great time in my life. I knew for sure that God, Source, That, was hearing my prayers. Yet I was becoming more and more skeptical of the people around me and their "so called" spiritual authority. My church was full of prophecy, "And thus and thus sayeth the Lord." It seemed as if now everyone had "a word" from the Lord.

My new apartment life on Avenue H was great. My roommate and I were getting along fine. But he was at a place in his life where he needed his space. He needed to get married, and he needed some room to find her. So, I decided to move out.

So, life went on, business as usual. Weekly church service was good. All was well. I made my move from my cool apartment in Midwood, Brooklyn, and I moved in with my Aunt Mary in the Bronx.

So, one day after the midweek church service in Manhattan, I was preparing to leave the church and jump on the 5 train, and I noticed Deacon Wineglass looking at me. He asked, "Peter, how are you getting home tonight?" I was kind of bitter from past experiences on the lifts home deal. So, I never expect anyone to give me a lift home. I always expect to take the train home. It was late and, besides, I now lived in Coop City. If I couldn't get folks to drop me in Brooklyn, where most of the members lived, I knew I couldn't get folks to drop me home to the Bronx. So, I answered him, "I'll be fine."

"Peter, how do you get home?"

"Deacon, I take a train and then walk home."

"Okay, Peter, take a different route tonight."

"Oh no, Deacon, I'm fine. I go home this way every night. I'll be alright."

He looked directly in my face with his dark, deep voice and said, "Go another way tonight."

Ugh, I respected him. But the only other way for me to get home without going my usual route would mean taking a cab, waiting for it, taking this long ride around the highway to get there, and spending money that I didn't have. No.

So, I took my same route, and then when I got off at Baychester Avenue, it started to bug me. The train ride home was exhausting. Sleepwalking down the ramp and out into the exit. I thought, "You know, it is kind of a risk walking over this bridge every night. Everyone else is crabbing up the cabs. Man, the bridge is right there. I go over the bridge every night. And there's always that feeling of "Man, this is a risk." But I always get home safe. Ay yi yi, the chaos to catch the last cab. Get it, get it, or you're going to have to wait for one of them cabbies to circle back. Aw man, the bridge is right there. Two seconds, and I'm home." Okay, now the train station had cleared. The last cab had gone out, and I was standing around looking stupid. The bridge was right there. I had lingered too long. "Okay, I'll just wait for the next cab." I waited. That took forever. Finally, a cab came back around. We began the journey home. It was way long and out of the way. You've got to be kidding me! People take this trip every day instead of walking over the bridge? This is crazy! I respected Deacon Wineglass more than any of the other church members. He was not a false prophet. He was the real deal. I only took the cab so that when he asked me if I took a different route that night, I could say, "Yes, I did."

The next day my aunt came in. "Peter, Peter, Peter!"

"What, what, what?"

"I told you to stop coming over that bridge at night. You see what happened?"

"No, what happened?"

"They murdered this young man on the bridge last night! He might have been coming through the same way you were coming through at night. I told you to stop coming over that bridge. You should see the blood all dripped down the stairs!"

"No way!"

"Yes, go and see! The news reporters and the cops and every-body were out there taking pictures."

"Wait a minute, let me go check this out. I can't believe my ears." So, I got dressed and ran over to the bridge to check it out. Sure enough, the steps on the bridge had big drops of blood all down the stairs leading back up onto the bridge. I walked up the bridge and over toward the middle dark spot. Wow, that could have been me. Obedience is better than sacrifice.

I am so glad that I listened to the nudging that said, "Oh, big deal, just do what Deacon Wineglass suggested." I am so happy that I didn't let ego get in the way. This could have cost me my life.

Thank God for a divine interception.

Coincidence:
A situation in which events happen at the same time in a way that is not planned or expected.
- The occurrence of two or more things at the same time
- The state of two or more things being the same

Miracle
- An extraordinary event manifesting divine intervention in human affairs.
- An extremely outstanding or unusual event, thing, or accomplishment
- Christian science: a divinely natural phenomenon experienced humanly as the fulfillment of spiritual law
- An extremely outstanding or unusual event, thing, or accomplishment

Christian science: a divinely natural phenomenon experienced humanly as the fulfillment of spiritual law.

The difference between coincidences and miracles is that miracles manifest divine intervention and fulfill spiritual law.

Now That I Know

Out on a Limb

Okay, now if I really shared with my friends and family some of the things that I've been experiencing, they would think that I'm crazy. People think I'm crazy already. I mean, think about it. Who has time to be walking through the streets praying in the daytime? The rest of the world is at their 9 to 5's. You're walking through the streets talking. If anyone saw me right now, they would definitely think, That guy is crazy and has escaped from the madhouse. Oh my God. I wish we had miracles like back in the Bible days. I wish I knew with certainty that I was not speaking out in vain. I wish that I somehow knew that praying out loud in the street is really communicating with God, Source, That. "God, please, if You are hearing me speak to You, please make that branch break off the tree."

The branch broke off of the tree and splattered right down in front of me. I stood there, stunned and amazed in the middle of the street, standing with my jaw dropped.

Yes, the branch broke off of that tree.

Yes, I am standing in front of a broken branch blocking my path to go forward.

I walked up to the roadblock and started to cry. That was the first time anything like that had ever happened to me. Okay, so I guess that was coincidental. Or was it a miracle?

My school friend Arlene introduced me to this book Out on a Limb written by Shirley MacLaine. Shirley MacLaine was living this kind of life that was intentional,

"Untitled"- Peter Anthony Moore's artwork

yet the divine intervention was beyond our finite mental understanding. My friend Arlene was adamant about how reading this book had changed her mind. I thought, Well, first of all, Shirley MacLaine is white, Shirley MacLaine is also a woman, and she's already rich. This whole thing is so far-fetched for me. But I thought, God, I wish I could live like that!

In this book Out on a Limb, she illuminated her journey of success in manifesting exactly what she needed in her journey and more. She rolled with the movers and shakers of the world in a real way. They were her extended family.

Four Seasons

My peeps, my New York peeps, the people who you deal with daily. My journey started with people who cater to the movers and the shakers of the world. They became my extended family. Joining the Four Seasons Restaurant was one of the best moves that I ever made. Alex Von Bidder is now much more than someone I worked for. He is now a real friend. The road was rocky and altogether magical all at the same time, just like Shirley MacLaine illuminated in her book Out on a Limb.

So, one day while working at the Four Seasons Restaurant, lo and behold, Ms. Shirley MacLaine came in to dine. She came in to dine right after a whole media hype over her book. She came to the front desk of the restaurant and asked me (the host) about her reservation. The mumbles and the grumbles and the whispers and snickering rose up all around from the James Beard room, through Picasso Alley, and all the way down to the pool room. The people were ridiculing her. I tried to look at her eye to eye. I was letting her know that the snickering didn't matter to me. She winced at me like she understood. I began to escort her down Picasso Alley. I try to keep small talk to a minimum when seating the Four Seasons guests. Most of the clients come to eat and do business. Her smile was warm and welcoming. But I could tell that she was being affected by all of the sneers, whispers, and snickering.

I wanted to let her know so badly that I was one of the dancers who had held her up doing the kick line in the celebration of the Statue of Liberty gig; but I didn't want to lose my job. She was definitely feeling the uncomfortable vibe from the guest as we entered the Pool Room. "Out on a Limb, sicko, crazy wackjob, nutcase." I walked her over to her table, acting like I couldn't hear the buzz. She was on table 63 next to Ms. Wusseldorf, an overly exaggerated cartoon character-type rich woman. She looked like the woman who always chased around Woody Woodpecker, trying to kiss him, "Woody! Woody!" That's exactly what she looked like. She flashed her diamond (supposedly she owned the biggest or the most diamonds in the world) ring and rolled her eyes at Ms. MacLaine. I pulled the chair for Ms. MacLaine and looked her in her eyes like, Please, I saw that. She's a snob. Then I spoke to her and told her to enjoy her lunch. I couldn't wait for her to finish her lunch so that I could escort her back through Picasso Alley, where I had escorted so many other people who I adore, like Bette Midler, Robert Schuller (my great-grandmother Mama Ifill watched him faithfully), Ruth Westheimer, Tracey Ullman, and even President Gerald Ford.

My favorite day at the Four Seasons Restaurant was the anniversary celebration of Rolling Stone magazine. I had no idea what I was in for. It was the first time that we had to set up coatrooms out into the lobby of the Seagrams Building. The excitement was in the air. Finally, the night started.

There is Jason Priestly. Man, I sure would like to work with him! 90210 is ending. OMG, there is Penny Marshall. I ended up working with her in The Preacher's Wife. OMG cool, she has on Converse, of course...oh, oh, here she comes! She wants me to carry her drink for her. Oooh. Cool, I hope she tips me. The place is getting so crowded. Let's get to the coatroom. They are probably swamped. Hey, there's David Bowie! He's definitely the life of the party. He's having a ball. Wow, all of these talented people.

This evening was an awards ceremony. They eventually all gathered in the Pool Room. The podium was in the center at the top of the stairs of the Paul Rosenquest Room. I was posted up at the workstation taking care of drinks with, I think, Lenny Kravitz (might have been someone else, not sure). Sitting near the pool was Don Johnson and Yoko Ono. Every presenter was stellar. Then the night really started to steam up. Billy Idol lit the night on fire. He got to the podium to receive his award. After accepting his award, he asked for his lovely wife Cindy Crawford to come up to the podium. When she started up the stairs to the Rosenquest Room, her dress totally illuminated. The lights on the steps made her dress see-through. The whole Pool Room gasped. Billy Idol looked out over the podium like, "What? What? What's going on?" She got to the top of the Rosenquest Room, and they seemingly began to fuss. Eventually, she was told that she had to step aside because the lights were making her dress see-through. The whole room was staring with jaws dropped. How embarrassing. She was standing up there smiling, clueless that all of her private parts were exposed. Talk about exposure! But, this was the incident that stole the show—show-stopper.

David Bowie took the stand. He had the crowd going. Everyone was drunk and tipsy now. He dazzled the crowd, taking them back through his successful musical ride. Iman was sitting at a center table facing the podium. Her hair looked like a giant Christmas tree. You couldn't miss her. David Bowie kept going on and on about his career. Then he said something like, "I don't know if it was when I became a woman." Iman's hair began to shake. Then he said, "Or when I was 'in between' trying to figure out what I was" or "when I was something in between." Well, anyway, that's rock and roll!

Iman exploded. She started to get up from her table...uh oh, bye, Lenny Kravitz! I think she's headed to the coat room. I started ahead of her toward the coat room. I looked back at her, and a media crowd with giant light bulbs was chasing behind her. She busted into the Seagrams lobby, furious. David Bowie came out behind her. "Hold on, hold on, calm down, honey!"

She yelled back at him; he flagged her off and headed back into the restaurant. She pulled out her ticket. I handed her her coat. There were giant light bulbs all behind her head. She turned around, and everyone started flashing lights in her face. She started waving and blocking her face as the reporters and photographers surrounded her. Andrew Stein (mayoral candidate at the time) made his way through the frenzy to try to save her from the crowd. He grabbed her arm to protect her. She slapped him right in the face, "Get your hands off of me!" David Bowie watched from the top of Picasso Alley and busted out laughing. She exited the Seagrams Building and left the anniversary celebration for Rolling Stone.

Wow, definitely one of the most magical nights of my life.

Live Your Dreams

C hristmas was always my favorite time of the year growing up. My best Christmas was when my godfather Bobby Estaven gave me my first bike. It was big and red, and it had tassels on the handlebars and a big bell in the middle. As I got older, I always used to look at the picture of that bike under the tree whenever I wanted to feel that way again. It was definitely a dream come true. I loved the smell of chestnuts roasting on the corners when my family and I braved it through the cold streets of New York just to see the windows at Saks Fifth Avenue and the giant tree at Rockefeller Center. But the big treat was right around the corner. Every year, my mother would get us tickets to see the Radio City Christmas show. We always had to wait outside on line for a long time to get in. But it was definitely worth the wait. When we got inside the fascinating theater, it was the biggest and the most fascinating theater that I've ever been in.

We made our way to the top of the theater. Everyone and everything looked so small from where we were sitting. I couldn't wait to get a chance to go to the bathroom because I could run real fast. So, when I got a chance to go to the bathroom, I was going to run down to the first level to see what it looked like from down there. I would fly down those stairs and go into the orchestra seat area. Wow, I wished we could afford to sit down there. I would always take a look up to see if I could see where we were sitting. Then after I got my fill of the orchestra view, I would run as fast as I could back to the top of the music hall and get back to my seat calmly as if I hadn't just taken a tour of the first floor. On my second bathroom break, I would go to the next floor, and then the next, and then the next. I loved running around Radio City Music Hall before the show began. But once the show began, I was affixed. I had waited all year for this. I loved when the orchestra started. That was also my mother's favorite part. Wow, look at all of those toys. Real kings from around the world came to Radio City with their animals just for us in New York every year. (You couldn't make me believe anything else!) I knew that because they were rich and had lots of jewels and crowns on stage. The whole experience was everything I had hoped for.

Years later, I was sitting in the orchestra with one of the choreographers (Linda Haberman). I started crying while watching the run-through of this magical show. She hugged me. "Are you okay?" I shared my childhood experience with her.

Here I am now, sitting in a private rehearsal for the show that I will now be performing in. I always dreamed of being on the stage with Santa when I was a child. Wow, now I will be one of the ones on the stage with all of the toys...and I now know that the animals definitely are real. Wow! I really, really made it.

It was coming close to showtime, and I still didn't have the xylophone securely. I was hoping that they would replace me. But they just kept looking at me like, "Come on, Peter, you can do it." It seemed like every rehearsal, I made a bad bong or a bing. You've got to be kidding me! It's close to showtime. I made so many mistakes, and they still aren't replacing me with someone who has played the xylophone before. Urgh. So, after a long day of rehearsal, I decided to try and get some time on my own. The xylophones were stashed away right near the camel's pen. She did not appreciate me practicing in her pen. It was disturbing and noisy. She let me know it. She kept trying to bite at me. But I couldn't go out on center stage at Radio City Music Hall and hit a wrong note. It just can't happen. I have to practice. She kept biting at me. Well, this ritual went on for some time until opening night. One day when I came into work, the animal trainer was exercising the animals on stage. This morning, she had the camel that was penned up next to the xylophones. When she saw me, she reacted. The trainer asked me what that was all about. I told her that she probably remembered me practicing next to her in her stable. She said, "Oh, okay, she's a good girl. I thought that that was pretty strange behavior for her. Stop it, Suzie. Hmm, that's odd, she's a good girl; anyways, have a good show!"

Then one night on stage, I was performing in the kings section, and lo and behold, who was on stage in front of me? The same camel that I had to dip and dodge from while practicing my xylophones was in front of me. The walk across the stage is slow and majestic. Suzie, I believe her name was, looked back and then double looked, like, "No way, there's that guy that I hate," and excreted her feces right in my path. Oh no, what am I going to do? Those little balls were rolling all over the place. Urgh. I tried to sneakily work my way around them without changing the choreography. I didn't want to get a note that I was doing something different. When I got to my final spot on stage, I looked over to the handler who had Suzie, and she was calming her down. As if making me walk through her mess wasn't enough, she started trying to spit on me. Everyone on stage in the nativity scene was laughing. These kinds of things always happen in the Christmas show year after year. They just didn't realize that this time, it was personal!

Every night, the Radio City staff would go outside to the line of the music hall and pick some lucky child to actually go on stage with Santa. That was the luckiest child in the world—he or she got to meet the real Santa! The other Santas were fake, but the one at Radio City Music Hall was the real Santa Claus, and you could tell because all of his reindeer were real. As a child, I always knew that it was always a set-up. How could they pick one child out of all of those children in the line? Now that I was actually in the show, I loved when this part of the show came. I couldn't wait to go over to that starry-eyed child and wow him or her with my robot skills during Toyland.

On this particular night, I was preparing for the show with a simmer down attitude. The wardrobe guy had put me through this whole ordeal that now had everyone looking at me kind of funny. I hated it. It turned me mad and cold. So, one of the dancers came in the dressing room and said, "Peter, the child that they picked off of the line says she knows you."

"Oh, please, don't even do it."

"I don't know—she looks like she could be related to you."

"Okay, I know what this is all about. This is all about getting me in a better mood because of what happened with the missing dance belt. She's a cutie. She's very talkative. Not only does she claim she knows me, she says she's related to me. Oh, okay, now you've overdone it. Guys, please, can I get ready for my show quietly? Thanks."

"Oh, okay, just saying, she's a cutie."

"Whatever."

While dancing Toyland, I usually did the same thing every night. So, on this special night of Toyland, I danced my way over to the child who had been picked to be on stage. I stuck my box robot head in front of the child like usual and, "Woah, Uncle Peter...OMG!"

"Blair?"

"Uncle Peter!" She got up from her seat in Toyland and started behind me, "Uncle Peter, Uncle Peter!"

I couldn't talk back because my mic was on. I tried to twist my mouth away from the mic so that I could tell her to go back to the sled, "Go back to the sled!" I couldn't believe it. Sure enough, it was my goddaughter on stage. What a magical moment. Not only did I get to do the Radio City Christmas show, but of all the children who come to the show, they actually picked my cousin off of the line to be a part of the Radio City Christmas Spectacular as well.

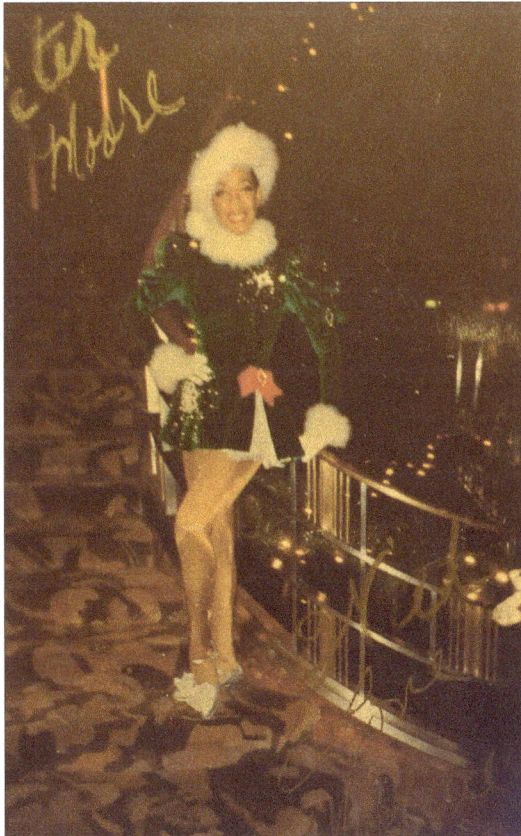

"A personal photo of my Rockette buddy Marque Munday."

Now unto him that is
Able to do exceedingly and abundantly more than we can think or imagine according to the power that worketh in us.

SMH...Les Brown
Let me tell ya, let me tell ya.

Now, I like reading inspirational books. So now everyone was going crazy about this new motivational speaker, Les Brown. My girlfriend started working with his seminars and was on the fast track to success. My mother lived near JFK Airport, which was where the seminar was being held. My girlfriend was assisting in the whole ordeal. This was a great career move for her. Les Brown bigged her up at one of his meetings at our church, St. Paul's Baptist in East New York Brooklyn. The excitement and the hype were awesome. It was so exciting. It made me consider following in his footsteps.

But is this the right thing for me? What will I gain out of following Les Brown? Will it produce any fruit in my life? At the end of the hoopla, where is the fruit? I got the book, Live Your Dreams. It was a working book with tests and questionnaires at the end of each chapter. I loved it. I did my assignments. It was very exciting.

So, while all engulfed in my Live Your Dreams experience, I met this guy named Terminator at the basketball courts at West 4th Street in the Manhattan Village. I just had to share with him my Live Your Dreams book experience. He was kind of bitter because he hadn't made it to the NBA. After listening to him and also watching the way he played the game, I shared with him that I believed that his gift was not on the court. Don't get me wrong, he was a baller. But his true gift was in his strategic mind. It was in his coaching and the love of the team. He was definitely a team player. I wanted him to realize the beauty of his gift. It was not all about him making the NBA. It was in doing exactly what he was doing. He kept others like him playing the game in basketball camps. He was a great coach. I encouraged him to embrace that.

I shared with him some of the juice I had gotten from my Les Brown book. He got so excited about Live Your Dreams. I was excited for him too. This book was a working book. The book had so much of my personal information on it at the end of each chapter. But I wanted him to get bit by the inspirational bug. So I lent my Les Brown Book Live Your Dreams to him so that he could catch a whiff.

Later on that week, I was doing some background acting on Spike Lee's movie Girl Six. I told my buddy Terminator about it. He told me to let him know when I was finished filming; He would come by and pick me up. So, at the end of the night, I was in the actors' holding area gathering up all of my stuff, preparing for my trip back to Brooklyn. Most of the other actors had signed out already. I walked out into the street and saw Terminator parked behind one of the production trucks. I took a second look, and sure enough, it was him. "Yo! What up, man?"

"I'll be out in a few. Let me just get everything together."

He noticed that I had a bunch of clothes. He said, "Pete, let me help you with that," and he stepped out of the car. When he got out of the car, the whole sidewalk on the other side of the street started shouting "Terminator, hey Terminator!" cheering and whistling. I was in total shock. I looked on the inside of the production truck, and Spike Lee was crouched down in the truck looking directly at me like, "Really?"

Oh my God, our holding area was on Christopher Street. All of the drag queens and gay men who lived there knew him from the basketball court. I was so embarrassed. I looked back inside the back of the production truck at Spike like I wanted to telepathically say, "Spike, it's not what it looks like." He looked back at me telepathically like, "Just pull out please." Christopher Street had the police bars up so they couldn't cross onto the set. But they were cheering and screaming for Terminator. I was devastated. My chances with Spike were now nil. Forget it. Terminator was smiling and happy like nothing had happened. I was embarrassed and kind of weirded out. We got into a conversation about it. He shared his love for them and how they made him feel. I felt like if he's going to be constantly hanging out with those guys that he might lose a lot of friends. Me, personally, I didn't want to be hanging out with him chilling and then here comes a bunch of loud drag queens screaming "Terminator!" and falling all over him. I felt like he might eventually have to ditch some of his drag queen friends. He was enraged with me. "Those are my friends, just like anybody else on the planet."

"I understand that. But in my personal experience, most of them don't like me."

"Well, I told one of them to come meet me here."

"Here where? At my house? Oh, hell no! I don't want no drag queens coming to my house. I don't want them to know where I live. Those guys don't like me."

"Oh, that is so wrong! I had it all wrong about you. You can forget about being my friend. Goodbye!" and he left, and so went my book. I never saw my book again.

In my book Live Your Dreams, I wrote out my five-year vision that came to fruition to the tee years later. I wrote in the book that I would like to originate in a black musical with black children's roles so that they could grow up and be famous and say that they played in this role as a child. I wanted to be in a musical that was cultural. I wanted to be in a musical where I would get the chance to fly. I was jealous that Scrooge from Radio City was white, and so was Peter Pan. I also wrote that I wanted to be living with the girl of my dreams in a property that I owned. Eventually, this is exactly what manifested.

Man! I wonder if Terminator is still around. It would be so amazing if he is alive somewhere, and he has my book Live Your Dreams. In that book is written in the worksheet section the blueprint for exactly what transpired later on in my life. He might or might not have my book. But I know what happened, and I remember what I wrote.

Don't let anyone steal your book!

The Jungle

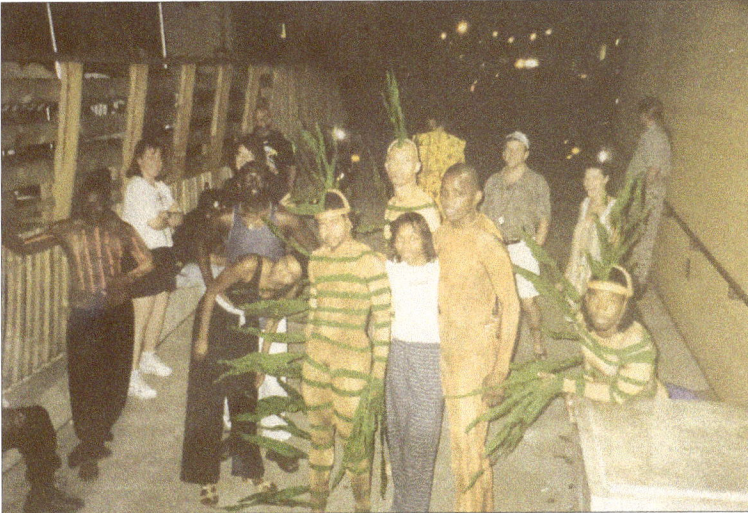

"A personal photo of lion king rehearsal break in Minneapolis"

when I decided to take on this journey of faith, I remember Pastor Lites letting me know that this walk of faith doesn't get boring when you commit to it. She told me that if I gave my life to Jesus, it would be so exciting beyond my wildest dreams...literally. And boy, did things get wild!

I agreed to go on the mission field with my pastor. The mission was going into Lima and Cusco, Peru. So far, nothing that I've experienced in my life has topped my Peru experience.

Yes, yes, yes, I went to Peru. The preparation was awesome. My church booked the trip with the company (Carrier Travel) that I worked for. Therefore, I had all of the best accommodations, no pay.

Briefing

We were told not to speak to anyone besides the pastors who our pastor introduced us to. We had to stay together and keep our eyes and ears open for instructions. We were told that we couldn't venture out alone. Stay in prayer always and don't speak, period.

The Plane Ride

The plane ride was the most magical plane ride that I've ever had in my life. The mountains were beautiful. There is an area along this air route known as the devil's triangle. So many planes have mysteriously disappeared. The tension was in the air. I had gained so much trust that my pastor was guiding us right that I wasn't fearful. The plane couldn't fly too high above the Andes or too low. We had to fly right in between. We were flying along, and then we passed a peak of a mountain beside the plane—so, so scary. The Andes were gorgeous. My stomach was in knots; turbulence was terrible. The church members were complaining and scared. Finally, we landed safe and sound in Peru. It was gray and foggy. The volcano had been smoking for the last couple of days, and the whole town was covered with gray volcano ash.

Welcome to Peru.

Guns were pointed at us from every angle imaginable. They were speaking harshly at us in Spanish. We were told not to talk to anyone. They (customs workers) were pressuring us to talk. I held my ground. Pastor Lites was in control. Then the family that we were so desperately waiting on showed up. It was so exciting to meet them. They checked us in, and the tension seized. The pastor who we were meeting was also the vice president of Peru. We were surrounded by national security the whole time. Guns were pointed at us from every area in the airport. We were still being checked out. The people of Peru loved their leader.

On my first morning after prayer, waiting for morning service to begin, I was sitting in the hotel lobby. I looked around, and sitting next to me was a jungle boy (exactly like the one in the Disney cartoon) okay. I looked back over at one of the pastors. He nodded to me like, "It's okay." I turned slowly back around, and Jungle Boy (Miguel) smiled, and his teeth were jagged. He was looking at me as if he wanted to eat me alive. He had the same complexion as the cartoon. His hair was pitch black and hanging just like the cartoon. I really couldn't believe my eyes. I looked back at the pastor. He looked back at me like, "It's okay." When I spoke, he imitated me immediately, staring intensely at my lips. He started to mimic everything that I did and said. We both were fascinated by each other. I wasn't afraid. He could speak a little English, Spanish, and all of the native Indian tongues. That's why he was with us, to interpret to the "uncivilized" Indians for Pastor. He had been sent by a group called "Youth with a Mission."

The Services Began

Doing the Pee wee Herman dance in Cusco Peru

40

He was by my side dancing with me the whole time.

Whenever "wild Indians" showed up, he interpreted for my pastor. Awesome! I asked him what it was like to live in the jungle. He said he lived day to day because when the government wants to kill them off, they just come in and do it and put up properties. I asked about the animals. He said when the people come in, the animals move out. Even living in the jungle, he said that a cat will pass through every once in a while. But if he just freezes, it will pass and let him go. Snakes are milling everywhere. They too move when he comes through. He said he was in the water washing off one day, and a snake began to wrap around him. He told me that he just bit it, and the snake let him go. Well, with those teeth! His main diet was monkeys and turtles, and he didn't expect to live past nineteen. If he did, he would know that he is a special one. I shared stories of when a loose German shepherd followed me across a busy highway and I got away. He loved that story, go figure. I eventually asked if I could visit his home in the jungle. Pastor said, "Are you crazy? Your family would kill me." It was way too dangerous. He said that the most dangerous threat of all is a poisonous ant. One bite, and you have minutes to get to the local witch doctor to remove the poison, or you're dead. This ant kills off most of the Indians who live in the Amazon. It was twenty-four hours by boat into the jungle, and I would have had to have a whole lot of government protection along with me. It wasn't happening. I cried when I left Peru. It was the most adventurous trip that I've ever had so far.

One of the best parts about it was that Pastor Juan really, really, genuinely loved me. I really didn't know until after the trip that he was actually the vice president of Peru…wow…out on a limb.

After this most amazing trip to Peru, it was back to work as usual. Back to sending out reports for Carrier Travel and daily church service at the Unbroken Chain.

My soul was so restless. I had stopped dancing professionally, and the only activities that I had were in the church.

Then one day when I was on my daily routine, I ran into George Faison. He looked at me in shock. I was chunky, and I was carrying a big briefcase. He said, "Peter, Peter, stop, stop...you at that church with CB and them?"

I said, "Yes."

He said, "You happy?"

"Very much so, praise the Lord!" My language had become churchy and robotic. George was looking at me as if he had just tasted something sour.

"Really?" he replied. I had been rushing when he stopped me, so I was ready to move on. He said, "You're not dancing anymore?" My answers were full of church lingo and very dismissive. But I told him no. He said, "Well, I have this Fred Astaire thingy that I want you to do, tap, real easy."

"George!"

"Can you tap?"

"Yes, George."

"Well just come over, and we'll talk about it. It's easy. I just need someone to help me with this thing. Come over to my house this weekend."

"I have church this weekend."

"Okay, after church."

So, the day came, and I went over to George's apartment. The first thing my eyes hit when I walked into his home was the Tony Award on the mantle. Did I say the Tony award on the mantle? My heart was shook. I was holding in tears. That day was the beginning of the rest of my life.

George and I were an awesome team. It began with me doing this little tap number. It turned into me assisting and learning production all engulfed and then eventually helping George out with the casting and running the auditions. I always looked up like "wow" at the auditioners whenever I went to an audition. Now for the first time in my professional dancing career, I was on the other side of the audition experience. My heart went out for my friends in the audition. But I really couldn't put a good word in for anybody. I would have tried if I could. Eventually I got to put my two cents in, but ultimately, it was up to George Faison. And this man knows talent. The show would become a medley of all the great movies of Hollywood. The owners of Peugeot showed up to see what George had lined up. Most of the groundwork was done. I was right beside George making sure he got his vision out to the Peugeot team as clearly as possible.

They liked my interaction with George. George was dramatic. I kept him cool. The vision was set. George needed people who really brought the essence of the movies we were depicting. One of the performers was so good. George fell in love with her and changed the whole image of Pretty Woman just for her. Julia Knight and I are still friends today. She got the show along with my buddy Danny from NCSA and one of my Chorus Line buddies Karl DuHoffman. George's chosen female assistant was everything. We all worked so well together. Yay! We were off to France.

Monaco

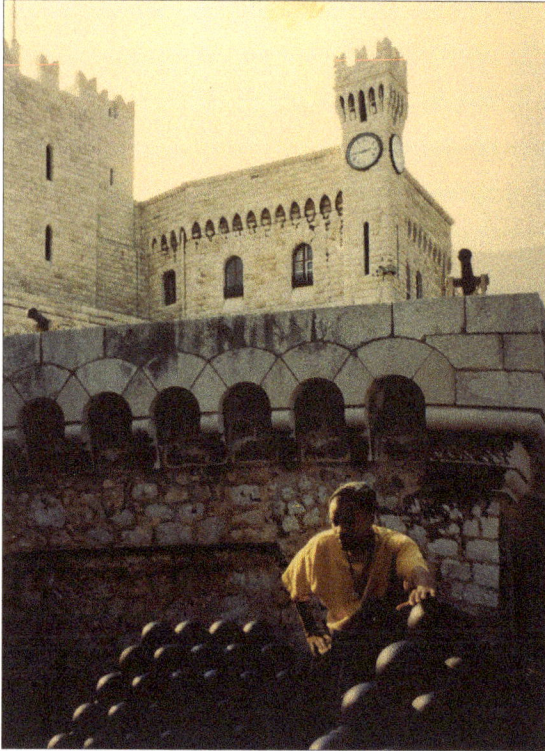

"Monaco"

Jullissa and I were roommates.

That ended on the first day. We loved the hell out of each other.

We somehow got all distorted about it on our first day in the hotel together. It was a distraction. She complained to T (George's better half).

They made accommodations for her to room alone. It was actually better for me. We had different interests. She wanted to hang out with George's crew, shopping on our downtime. I was fascinated with France. I ventured out on my own.

"Jullissa"

"OUT ON MY OWN"

The president of Peugeot asked me if I was having a good time. He liked my fascination with France. He offered to show me around. He drove me around and showed me all of the palaces of Monaco and gave me their history. Then he took me to this big, giant casino. I couldn't believe my eyes. Everything was so beautiful beyond my imagination. We entered the casino. We got our drinks. He told me to have a seat outside of the gambling area while he went inside to take care of some business. I sat at a small table for two, wide-eyed and amazed as I sipped on my amaretto sour. Mr. Peugeot had walked me into the casino. Everything was so surreal. I slowly slipped back down to earth to notice whom I was sharing this table with. When I looked across from me, I came eye to eye with President Gerald Ford. I turned back around quickly to compose myself. I wanted to tell him that I was the same guy (host) who had held the doors of the Picasso Alley for him while I was working at the Four Seasons. When I about-faced, his face was in shock. His face looked like he had seen a ghost. He looked at Mr. Peugeot as to say, "What is this outrage?" Mr. Peugeot jumped in, "Oh, this is Peter Moore He is one of the performers in the show that we are presenting at the sporting club." President Ford looked at Mr. Peugeot in his face like, "What the hell?" and quickly got up and made his way onto the gambling floor. I walked back with Mr. Peugeot to the gambling room. I couldn't understand the game, but every once in a while, a chip would fall on the floor near my foot. Then someone would snatch it up.

I asked Mr. Peugeot how much each chip was worth. He told me that each chip was worth about $5,000. Wow! See, venturing out on my own was way better than going with the crowd.

I had my own room too. This was heaven. My hotel room was simple. It was one of the most beautiful hotel rooms that I had ever been in. It was on a corner of the building on the edge of a cliff. The whole wall was glass. When I pulled open my windows, all I could see were blue skies and blue seas.

We were getting close to showtime, so we moved over to the (I believe it was called) Beach Plaza Hotel, right on the water next door to the Monaco Sporting Club. On our first lunch together, I thought, "Oh no, if they are going to be feeding us like this every day, I am going to lose my six-pack!" The food was delicious, but it was French. We were served steak and beef with heavy cream sauces, breads, and plenty of wine. We had our meals set out for us daily.

I got up from my delicious lunch and went into the bathroom. When I stepped away from the toilet, I heard a buzz, and then the toilet folded up into the wall, and I heard washing like at the car wash. I stood in the stool amazed with my mouth open and hand on my heart. The toilet then slowly came back out of the wall without a toilet seat on it. And then a new toilet seat wrapped in plastic slowly covered the face of the bowl. OMG. No way. Yes way.

They say that Monaco is where the whole concept of the Bond movies started.

It gets better. So, we signed into our hotels and checked into our rooms. The beach was beautiful. The water was so clean and crystal clear. This would be my reality for the rest of the trip... wow! So, I got a towel and laid out on the sand. A waiter came over. "Can I get you something to eat or a drink from the bar?" Oh, yes! Loving this. They had these mini pizzas that looked so delicious.

"You know what? Can I have a pizza and a Coke?" Before you knew it, I looked up, and the waiter was walking toward me with a little table on his arm arrayed in a red and white checkered cloth. He placed the little table down besides where I was sunning. He secured the table sweetly in the sand, and then he put the red and white plaid tablecloth on top and served me my soda in a fancy glass with a straw.

The pizza was not the New York sloppy kind with cheese and sauce dripping everywhere. This pizza was very thin crusted, the special tomato sauce kind, hmmm, not too filling. Then I got the bill. $33, you've got to be kidding me! For that little piece of pizza and that sip of Coke? Okay, I guess I'll be eating the food provided!

Our hotels were paid for too. We were responsible for any other miscellaneous charges. The rehearsals were magnificent. The show was coming together wonderfully. It was a challenge for me to help everybody with his or her parts, rehearse the cast, and keep it tight so that George didn't lose his mind, on top of keeping myself together for my part in the show.

I would get up wee early in the morning to get away from the cast and George and go to the gym. This was the most beautiful gym that I've ever been in, to date. The pool was like a giant seashell. The water was mineralized. On the decks of the pools were Turkish baths available for you to sweat. Gym assistants were ready at hand to accommodate your every need. I began to take full advantage. This meant that I had to get there way before my rehearsal schedule to get back in time to work.

I would get into this very private workout room with glass walls on the edge of the mountain looking out to the sea. One other guy would be there with me every morning. Allison Williams (R&B singer) asked me if I could give her a workout in the mornings. I told her that I could do it after my own personal workout. I told her that the gym was very private and quiet. There was only this one guy in the workout room with me. So, Allison and I made out our regiment.

So, I was on my daily routine, and the other guy in the gym and I began to talk. I know that I was not what he was expecting to see in the gym. He asked me what I was doing in Monaco. I told him that I was performing at the show at the Sporting Club. He was fascinated and asked me about the dancing. I showed him some of my stretches. Allison and I would then link up in another private room so that I could give her her personal warm-up.

So, this one day, Allison stuck her head in the room where me and this guy were working out. She was letting me know that she was ready and waiting for me in the other room. When I looked over to Allison, her giant big brown eyes got even bigger. "Peter, Peter, is that your workout partner?"

"Yes."

"Is that who you have been working out with for the past week?"

"Yes..."

"Peter, don't you know who that is?"

"No, who is that?"

"Peter, that's Ringo!"

"Oh, really...cool." I didn't know who Ringo was. So, it didn't really faze me. I was too engulfed with the show. When I later found out who I had been working out with, I was beside myself. I was elated. Thank you, God. I love his music. Ringo Starr. OMG.

Thank God for George Faison. He put me back on the performing path again.

Eventually I ended up leaving the Unbroken Chain church. It was one of the hardest things that I had ever done. I would be sitting in church, dancing and choreographing and visualizing the whole message through. But then year after year, I wasn't gaining any ground in my life.

So, five years later, I decided to go back into show business full force. Thank God that George saw something in me that I couldn't see in myself.

I kept fantasizing about moving to Los Angeles. So, one day, I decided to use my benefits from working with Carrier Travel and go and check out Los Angeles. I took my buddy Epperson with me.

He was pushing his hats. We didn't tell the pastor that we were going. We got in so much trouble, but we had such an adventurous time. I definitely got bit by the bug. The Black Hollywood Film Fest was my next move. The trip was good. But the remix was when I ran into my sister Gwen McGee. She laid the "LA game" down to me. "If you're going to move over here, it's like this, and it's like that." She showered me in wisdom and love. She told me about her church in LA, and on the Sunday before I went back to New York, we visited. When I got to the entrance of the church, I heard, "Namaste." I felt so welcomed, I couldn't believe it. It was one of the women from St. Paul's Church in Brooklyn. The church was so warm and welcoming. It was like an oversized St. Paul's in Los Angeles. OMG. This is it. I think I'm going to make this move, and I found my new church already.

Los Angeles

You Make Me Hot

My intro to work life in Los Angeles was awesome. My buddy Kenny suggested that I would be a good replacement for Desmond Richardson for the AMA's. The audition was so fascinating. The Los Angeles dancers were "off the chain". They had style, flair, and beauty. They were full-out performers. Their audition gear was outrageous. It was showtime.

I looked like I had just finished giving them a class. This was definitely new for me. I really didn't feel the angst that the other auditioners were having because I knew that I was a good technical dancer. I had pirouettes and splits. These dancers had the hip-hop thing down. I was watching them and picking up moves and styles that I would now add to the routine that I normally wouldn't have done. I'm a technically trained dancer. I have a good eye. I could turn on a dime, and I had the combination. But Frank Gaston (the choreographer) wasn't feeling me. "He is not Desmond." So now, I wasn't feeling so secure. I was staying with my buddy Tai. So, when I got back to Tai's apartment and shared all that had happened, he jumped right in, trying to hook his buddy up. I had to jazz it up and hip-hop it. So, I got one of his shirts and some better dance pants and went back with a new look out of Tai's closet. Frank threw his hands up (uh oh). He turned us (my audition group) over to the Braxton family. He said he only wanted the people who go for the blood. All others would be cut. The Braxtons agreed. It was on.

Each group came out amazing with their new outfits, techniques, tricks, flips, hair pieces, heels, splits, and everything else. Okay, it was my turn to go. I had done stolen enough moves, nuances, and flavorings from the previous groups. So, now I got my pirouettes and my splits and my new secret sauce weapon. Five, six, ready, and I came out. I felt good. Tai's oversized silk shirt was working. I saw that Toni Braxton and her family were liking me. I went in on my improv moment, pirouettes split, and then my secret sauce weapon move. When I did it, the whole room screamed out, "Yeah! Work, work!" One of Toni Braxton's sisters said, "Yes!" pointing at me, "He is too cute." I felt like a million bucks. I looked over at Frank Gaston's face, and he rolled his eyes like, "Please."

Yeah, man, I got it. Rehearsals with Dick Clark, backstage with Sinbad, performing with millions, what a dream come true. BUT, oddly enough, I came to this understanding early. I came to the understanding that right then, I was not supposed to stay here in LA. Check out how it happened. During my visit with my buddy Tai, it just seemed like we weren't vibing right. I felt like I was invading his space. I felt sad. I was looking out of his window. For what? No one walks the streets in LA. They're all in their cars. This was really a different world. Heavy-hearted and kind of sad, I looked around, and there was this beam of light coming through the window. It was a sunray beautifully shaped like a theater spotlight. I followed the spotlight, and it made a perfect circle right on my music book and audition material by Tai's piano. It read Jesus Christ Superstar, Peter Anthony Moore On Broadway. When I took it in, I had a chill. There was this perfect spotlight on my headshot that's reading "Jesus Christ Superstar, Peter Anthony Moore, On Broadway." I still get chills when I think back about that moment. I was stilled, in awe, on my knees, staring at my headshot with my hand on my heart.

Peter Anthony Moore…Jesus Christ Superstar…On Broadway…hmmm?

Soooo…

- Don't let anyone talk you out of your miracle.

King of New York

So, I got back to New York and kept it moving, back on the New York grind. I knew that I wanted to make that move to Los Angeles. But this wasn't the right time.

So, I went in for the new year of the Radio City Christmas show. It's supposed to be a shoe in once you've done the show the year before. But I had some crazy incidents that changed the game. The tragic day when the wardrobe guy tried to play a silly joke. He didn't pre-set my dance belt for the show. So, while preparing to go on for the Christmas show, I noticed that my dance belt wasn't set. I ran all over the theater looking for the wardrobe guy. He couldn't be found. I ended up missing my cue to go on. One of the dance assistants ran on stage and did my bit in his jeans. This was a final run through with a live audience for the producers of the show. Press were there taking pictures for the media. The reporters caught a shot of me running around backstage in my dance belt looking for the wardrobe guy. Disaster. The next day, a huge commotion and meeting proceeded. What happened?

Everyone was chiming in. But most importantly, all of the Rockettes stood up for me and told management that I was going crazy backstage trying to find the wardrobe guy, and he was nowhere to be found. He had been hiding from me and thought that the whole thing was funny. This wardrobe guy was everybody's favorite buddy. But this time, the games went too far. He got fired, and everybody hated me for that. So when I walked in to be put in for the next year's show, everyone snarled at me. The auditioner looked over at me and said, "Well, I just want to let some of you know, the show is overcasted this year, and some of you who were in the show last year are not guaranteed a place in the show this year." Then she glared at me like, "Yeah, you." Uhh, see what this damn wardrobe guy done done?

They hated me now, and as it is, I am way too short for the show. I really got in on Bobby Lindgren's favor because I had just come off the road with him in A Chorus Line. Damn, I might not be able to get this money like all of the other dancers I know, folk who do it year after year, and at Christmas time, they always have their money. Damn, who cut the cheese? This stinks. Can you smell it?

Well, I jumped in, and the audition process started. We had all learned the routine, and it was time to audition; the auditioner stopped the usual process and made an announcement. She announced that these particular men who had already been stars on Broadway had to audition first and then leave because they had a special call for The Lion King for the role of Simba. She announced that one of these guys was going to be our Simba on Broadway. I was amazed. I watched them with so much respect and envy.

I recognized one of the dancers from Cats. He was an amazing performer, wow. I didn't recognize the other guys. But the whole room applauded when they finished the combination. Um, but I wasn't too impressed. They really didn't impress me. Wow, and one of these guys was going to play Simba? My stomach was already shot by the way that I had been greeted by the auditioner. They ain't letting me back in.

The Simba guys finished their audition, and then they began to exit with everyone applauding them.

I decided to make my exit; I knew that they weren't going to put me back in the show. So, as those guys were gathering their things, I gathered my things as well and left out with them and came out the backstage entrance of the Radio City audition as if I was together with them in this Simba group. When we all got outside together, they started talking about what the agent had told them to do.

They started, "He told us to go to this location, got it, go to this floor, got it, all the audition details got it." The group broke up. Two guys caught a cab. The others decided to walk. I followed them to the private audition spot. I moseyed around and then went into the bathroom to listen. They walked over to the agent's office and got all that they needed for the audition. Then they left to prepare for the audition. They all went their own special ways, coffee and bagels, and so on. When the coast was clear, I came out of the bathroom. I went over to the agent's office door. The door was locked. I jimmied it a little with my Actor's Equity union card, and the door came open. I walked over to the desk, and there on the desk was the list of the guys who were coming to the audition with their info on a card. Think quick, think quick.

I started to write a note to the agent. I wanted to let him know that I had been in Los Angeles during the whole audition period and missed all of the auditions. Was it at all possible that I could somehow audition for the show today? While I was writing the note on the desk, the doors came flying open. Oh my God, busted!

"What in the hell are you doing in here? You are trespassing. What are you doing in my office, and what the hell are you doing at my desk?" Others walked in behind him in shock. I started trying to talk quick, and then Lebo, the guy who ran the one day workshop that I got from The New York Times paper stepped forward.

He said "Hold on, wait a minute, I saw this guy before."

The agent said, "This is not one of my clients. I don't know what he thinks he's doing."

Lebo said, "Wait, I saw him before. He came to the workshop with a beautiful girl with red dreadlocks in her hair."

Then Garth Fagan walked in the room. "What is all of this? Wait. Don't I know you? Didn't you used to dance for Alvin Ailey?"

I said, "Yes, yes."

Julie Taymor said, "Wait a minute, you know him?"

Garth said, "Yes, that's Peter. That boy can dance."

The agent said, "Well, the dance auditions are over. This is a special call for Simba. All of my guys have a certain vocal range, and besides, the show has already been casted. All of these guys have been stars on Broadway."

Julie Taymor said, "Oh my God, big deal, we only have an hour. Stick him on the back of the line and let him audition."

The agent was furious.

Yay, I was going to audition! So, although these guys were singers, they wanted to see if these guys could move. Garth gave a very long, hard modern dance combination. The guys were fuzzy. They definitely didn't have it, neither did I, but there was an attitude turn and a pench'e (leg up in the back making a straight 180-degree angle) at the end of the combination, my specialty. Then he put on the music. I couldn't believe it. It was "Brown girl in the ring, tra la la la la. Brown girl in the ring traaaa, la la la la la."

I knew every lick and tick of this song. I grew up on this music. So, I started to wine up. Julie Taymor looked at the others like "Hold on, he knows this song." The combination was long. They danced the combination as much as they could remember to the song. The guys were going for it; they were all good performers. Some of them had really good memory. But the execution was way wrong, offbeat, and really just not good, wrong flavor. These were basically good singers. So, when I got up to dance, I decided not to hold back and show them that I could really dance. When I did the pench'e (180-degree ballet move) at the end of the combination, Garth Fagan and Julie Taymor's eyes popped open wide, and they simultaneously shouted, "Wow, beautiful!" The agents were furious. So now that part was over. Here we go, we were getting ready to sing. The agent came out and started to talk about the lineup. I looked over to him as if to ask a question.

He snarled at me, "Not you, I'm talking about the real auditioners. You will audition when they have all sang." The guys lined up to sing. They sounded like the best opera singers you could have ever heard. I listened by the door. I heard Lebo (Lion King's music man) complain about each guy. He said, "I asked that the guys bring in material that was pop. I don't want to hear opera; this is not the sound of the show." Think quick, Peter, think quick. I had my Jesus Christ Superstar music book on me. That's it, I'll sing that and just speed it up.

So, they called me into the room.

I walked over to the piano and gave over my music. The piano player started to ask questions about the speed and the key. I pointed to the key I wanted him to play, and then I did a hand bone for the speed. When I looked around, the auditioners were cracking up. The hand bone had broken the ice. Once I started to sing, I knew that I had them.

I started my song "Jesus Christ Superstar" like Michael Jackson doing "Billie Jean. The demonstrators for the dance combination were peeing their pants. The whole room was cracking up. The two agents were furious and not laughing. Julie Taymor's face was unforgettable. She looked at Lebo and Garth and said, "I think we found our Simba," and lo and behold, I landed my first Broadway show, The Lion King.

I got the show!

But not so fast, partner. They called me up with this whole story. "We have to figure this out. We just cannot give you Simba. Have you ever been on Broadway before?"

"No."

"Okay, okay, hold up." So, they invited me to a private office on Park Avenue. They were looking at me in such amazement. They loved what I had accomplished through my audition, but everything had to be right. Basically, I got into the show through a private audition. They couldn't honor me with the Simba role, even though I had outshined all of their chosen Simba's. I eventually agreed to a swing contract.

Yay, I had a contract, and I was off and running. Rehearsals at the infamous 890 Broadway every day except Sundays, let's go. Then we were off to Minneapolis to put up the show. Hold on, not so fast. "Hi, Peter, you have been chosen to star in this independent film Blind Faith."

"Oh wow, really, when is the audition?"

"There is no audition. You have been chosen."

"OMG, I just got Lion King!"

"It's only a week-long shoot in Toronto."

Okay, okay, you got this. It's all going to be okay. I'm sure Julie Taymor would understand. "Hi...Julie, is it possible that I take a leave from rehearsals for a week to tape Blind Faith?"

"Absolutely not! When you came back, you definitely would not know the show."

I cried my eyes out. I would have been working with Courtney Vance and Forest Whitaker. Ya, can't do both. Swallow the pill. So, I settled in in Minneapolis.

The stage was amazing. I hung out at the club First Avenue where Prince first played. I busted out on my own and was loving it.

Julie Taymor had a vision with these stilts on the giraffes. She wanted someone to try something for her. So, I went on stage unrehearsed, walking on stilts for the first time for Julie. I fell on those stilts in Minneapolis because I had never learned to walk on stilts. I just assumed I could do it. Plus, I wanted Julie Taymor to know that she didn't pick no chump.

"ON THE STILTS"

So, I jumped up on the stilts untrained in front of an audience and busted my behind. That set the fear in. I busted my butt on them stilts a couple more times before I really became secure. It was a rough, rugged journey. But before you knew it, I was "Boagalin" on them stilts during the bows.

I was in the grove of my Broadway show as if I had been born to do it.

I remembered Pastor Maria talking about her call to per-forming artists. She believed that if she could just shake hands with some of them (celebrities, politicians, rich and famous) that she could pray for them. I said to myself that it would be a dream for me to be able to make contact like that with them. I dreamed of praying for all of those rich and famous celebrities just that way. I understood my pastor's passion for them because I myself have some sort of unexplainable love for them as well.

I ended up shaking hands and getting my blessings to President Clinton.

The whole Democratic party came to the show. Stephen Spielberg, George Lucas, Robin Williams, Harry Belafonte, Sidney Poitier, Sting, John Travolta, Nicholas Cage. Robert Townsend

John Singleton

The most special moment for me was when DMX
came through because alot of people came backstage every
night and were waiting on stage to meet the cast. A lot of the time,
I didn't know who the actor was. That didn't mean anything to
me. They probably acted on a show that I didn't watch. So that
didn't mean anything to me. But DMX was special to me. When
he first came out on the music scene, he came out covered in
"the blood." That was so special to me. It was as if he came out
covered in the blood of Jesus. As his career grew, I recognized his
faith connection, and best of all, he made music that I listened to.
The stage manager of the show was trying to close up the theater
and get everybody home.

DMX

He was on stage and fascinated. Do you know how much I loved that moment? He probably thought that I was kind of crazy. I probably had leftover makeup from the show on my face because I had rushed on stage to see him. Although the stage manager had closed up the office, I made sure she didn't play herself, and she reopened the office and got a good marker for DMX to sign the famous celebrity wing that all of the politicians and celebrities signed when they came to see the show.

That's right, one of my favorite rappers came to see my show. We met, hung out for a minute, and I made sure that that celebrity signed our famous Lion King wing.

Muhammad Ali asked me, Who's greater than God and badder than the devil?"

I looked up at him like, "I don't know."

In his still swaggerific shaky voice, he said, "...Nobodyyyyy!"

OMG. I met the man Muhammad Ali.

So, one night after the show, I was making my way out into the audience through the cast's private alleyway when I noticed someone in there walking toward me. It was totally dark and very narrow. I could only see some sparkles moving toward me. So, I walked backwards slowly into the light, and the sparkles lit up and opened to that big, giant smile of Diana Ross. I gasped! Then I said, "I've waited for this moment my whole life!"

She replied, "Well, here I am!" She hugged me and then asked me to show her around backstage. Of course, that was my favorite moment of all. It was all like one big spectacular blur.

Now unto him that is

Able to do exceedingly and abundantly more than we can think or imagine according to the power that worketh in us.

The desert of the whole ride was

My Boo Cat

A little tapioca. Just a little, and some Bombay sapphire.

In the midst of it all, yes, yes, yes, I had a heart-ripping, soul-sipping, knock down, dragged out love affair. When she came to the cast of Lion King, Doc (stage manager) brought her to the male dressing room door, and she stuck her head in and said hello. I was struck. I dropped my head on my desk thinking of her. Then I heard my buddy Ashi screaming, "Peter, Peter, Peter!" and then all of the guys went off yelling and cheering and talking at the same time.

My buddy Michael stopped the noise, "Stop, stop, stop. Peter, did you hear what we just said?"

I said no.

They all started yelling and talking at the same time. Mark Davis said, "No way, you heard what we just said, yes you did!" I didn't hear what they were talking about. They went off. The dressing room went crazy.

"I've never seen him like this before," said Ashi. OMG, I was dumbstruck. When we went into rehearsals and began the whole process of putting her into the show. I felt so discombobulated. I was struck. When rehearsal was over, she asked if I could take her to the Village. She had always wanted to see Soho. What a day. We went into the Village together. We were getting to know one another. We had some of the same tastes and likes. She was so excited to see NY Village and Soho. I loved that I was the first one to show her New York's Village and Soho communities. But when I got back to work, I couldn't stop thinking about her. Other guys in the cast were scheming. I told her that I'd show her any of New York that she wanted to see. Then she told me that she was going out for drinks with one of the other cast members. Yuck. I stepped back. I could see in her eyes that she didn't want to go with him. She wanted to be with me. I surely was not going to go out for drinks with the cast with this guy escorting her around. So, one day on that nightly ritual that started, I asked her if she wanted to see Brooklyn. BAM! That ended the other guy's foolishness. She came home to Brooklyn with me, and that became the beginning of us.

"OMG, what are we doing?"

"...Uhhh, having a beer on my fire escape on Warren Street." We both swallowed the pill. "We adore each other. That's it, you're moving in." And that's when heaven began.

I was so accustomed to living by myself. I came in from work, and there were flowers on the center table. The bathroom was beautiful with towels and soaps that I love, and everything was so clean. The bed now had sheets on it. Boo cat's colors, mint green and lilac. What a dream come true. Doing Lion King with her now as my girlfriend really changed it all. I was swamped with the show, but I now had a dream girlfriend.

When I was younger watching basketball games with the other men in the family, I loved when the cheerleaders came out. And I always thought, Man, why can't I have a girl like that? 'And sure nuff, Boocat used to be a Lakers cheerleader.

The moon kissed us in Hawaii. We had a magical time together. Fellow cast member Levensky threw the baddest going away party on a ship when he left The Lion King. Dameka and I danced into oblivion. We had Valentine's day at the Sugar Shack with Ashford and Simpson. We attended the Acapulco Film Fest together. I was so in love with her.

A little tapioca. Just a little, and some Bombay sapphire.

Now unto him that is

Able to exceedingly and abundantly more than we can think or imagine according to the power that worketh in us.

Oh, by the way, I was one of the select few out of the Lion King cast chosen to sing the United States national anthem at the opening of the Yankees season.

It Just Happened

42nd Street Blueprint

Somebody else saw it. I ran into the woman who used to preach in Times Square with her husband with ceramic lungs and hearts and gross pictures preaching doom and gloom to the passersby. I ran into her yesterday, Friday, July 9, 2015. I began to share with her the miracle of the blueprint. I thought she was going to be all crazy. But she was warm and sweet. She started to remember when I began to recall that night.

We had been sitting at the same table in a chicken rotisserie spot around 43rd and 9th avenue. She said, "Oh yeah, that was a long time ago." I asked her if she remembered the night that we were sitting there when suddenly, this man came rushing in. He went to the back corner with a blueprint in his hand. He called the cook over, "Hey you, believe this shit? Yeah man, they are trying to put all of the porn shops off of 42nd. What's your dad gonna do? He's talking about going down to the meat market. Here, here, look at this."

The street evangelist and I lifted our eyes from our meals and humbly took a glance. He pulled out the blueprint for the new 42nd Street. I thought to myself, Now, that's crazy, the "E" walk? That looks like Disney World to me. I finished off my food and left.

"Do you remember that?" Wow, sure nuff, she remembered.

Now, here's the crazy part. I was beside myself on that night that I was recalling to the Times Square evangelist. I was sexually frustrated and crying out to God on 42nd Street. I was crying and praying because I couldn't resist the temptations of 42nd Street. I was way too vulnerable. If there was only one peep booth to go in after work, that was the one that I was trying to get through. It was only a quarter for a couple of minutes of porn. And if you went in the one where it had a side window, it slid up so you could peep at the person on the other side. I just kept getting in trouble. It was driving me crazy. So on this particular night, by the newsstand on the corner of 42nd and 7th, I cried out to God, Source, That. I spoke honestly through my great intercessor Jesus. I admitted that the temptations were too much for me to handle. "Dear God, would You change this for me?" I heard, "Yes." Immediately, before I could go on pleading in my prayer, my mind shifted and said, "Yeah right, Peter, you're talking to yourself." I glanced up at the activities across Times Square that were tempting me. I knew that if I had the money to go across the street and engage, I would. It was all too much. All the trains passed through 42nd Street. I had to pass through this daily.

After crying out to God, Source, That, I walked down to 8th Avenue and walked over a couple of blocks to the chicken rotisserie. That's when the man with the new 42nd street blueprint in his hand came busting into the chicken joint. Now, remember, I had just come off of 7th Avenue, praying for change on 42nd Street moments ago.

Now, here he came in right after with the new 42nd Street blueprint in his hand. OMG, really?

Coincidence or miracle?

To top it all off, I was still in awe that I actually got to recall that miraculous night with the crazy Times Square evangelist who was actually there when the blueprint man showed up. She ain't that crazy. She remembered that night. Awesome...God is so good.

So, now years later on my journey, I got a call from an old friend, Al. He said, "Hey Pete, I was walking down 42nd Street and saw your name up in lights." I thought to myself, What? What are you talking about? So, night after night while I was performing in The Lion King, I would go to work and get off the train at the same exit. I would also go home the same way.

So, after Al told me that he was walking down 42nd Street and saw my name up in lights, I had to check it out for myself. So, instead of going home the same way, on this night, I decided to see what Al was talking about. So, I walked around to the corner of 42nd, and I looked up, and lo and behold, there it was. My name was on the marquee on the corner with the rest of the cast of The Lion King. But the way it was placed, it was if my name was highlighted. My name was splattered out right in the middle. I stared at the marquee in unbelief. Then my eyes opened up to the rest of the block, and I remembered the blueprint.

There it was, manifested right before my eyes.

Answered prayers.

Coincidence:
A situation in which events happen at the same time in a way that is not planned or expected.
- The occurrence of two or more things at the same time
- The state of two or more things being the same

Miracle
1 An extraordinary event manifesting divine intervention in human affairs.

2 An extremely outstanding or unusual event, thing, or accomplishment

3   Christian science: a divinely natural phenomenon experienced humanly as the fulfillment of spiritual law

The difference between coincidences and miracles is that miracles manifest divine intervention and fulfill spiritual law.

Boatyard Blessings

So, wow, I was on Broadway, and I had a paid vacation, and I was in Barbados at The Boatyard with my cousins having the time of my life. My dream was to be on Broadway. The second part of that dream was to see my grandmother sitting in the audience. Man, my grandmummy was gone. On the day of her death, I was in my Aunt Mary's apartment alone praying, praying for peace in my heart. I was so confused as to why God would let my grandmother go. I was crying out for a word from heaven for comfort.

I grabbed my Bible, and I started to throw about the pages. "Please, Jesus, speak to me. Please, Jesus speak to me."

Ephesians 3:18: "May be able to comprehend with all saints what is the breadth, and length, and depth, and height."

I believe my grandmother wanted me to continue in my faith walk. She wanted me to continue for real. To walk genuinely and honestly in this faith journey so that I would know it for real. If I am to really know what this faith walk is all about, it's going to take some pain.

No Pain, No Gain.

I went out to the back of the bar. It was a magical night. I knew better than to go playing in the water because I knew these waters. Sea life in Barbados is no joke. I walked over to the shore and looked up into the sky. The night sky was beautiful. The bar was bouncing. Wow, I felt so good. I had a good drink in my hand. Everyone was partying, and no one was paying attention to me. I took the opportunity to sing out loud to God. I sang

Endless Night" (Simba's song). I sang it in pain because I was now in the show, and I was not playing the role of Simba or singing this song for anyone. I sang, but it was a sad song. When I finished singing, I heard a soothing beat from the bar. The beat caught my attention. The beat that came from the bar that still sometimes makes me shed a tear. It was Sting, "Every breath you take, every move you make, every vow you break, I'll be watching you." I knew my grandmother was speaking to me. I started to cry. So, if she was watching, I wanted to show her something. So, I decided to start dancing along the shore. I heard my cousin Cathy scream out, "Go, Peter!" I danced some more and made my way back over to the bar.

It was one of the most memorable moments of my life.

Now, was it a coincidence that Puffy decided to remake Sting's song in tribute to Biggie Smalls, and then the boatyard DJ decided to play it at the exact moment when I was at the back of the boatyard in Barbados trying to find solace around my grandmummy's absence? I don't know, you decide. The whole experience was a chain of miracles. Sean Puffy Combs got inspired at a very painful time in his life. He had lost one of his best friends. He was inspired to remake the hit song in the spirit of emotional healing. The ripple effect blessing continued onto me like the waves from the sea at the shore of the boatyard in Barbados.

I saw Puffy in a different light from that day forward because I don't believe in coincidences. Puffy is a messenger of God. Not for nothing, but I heard he came from a traditional church-loving home.

Coincidence:
A situation in which events happen at the same time in a way that is not planned or expected.
- **The occurrence of two or more things at the same time**
- **The state of two or more things being the same**

Miracle
1 **An extraordinary event manifesting divine intervention in human affairs.**
2 **An extremely outstanding or unusual event, thing, or accomplishment**
3 **Christian science: a divinely natural phenomenon experienced humanly as the fulfillment of spiritual law**

The difference between coincidences and miracles is that miracles manifest divine intervention and fulfill spiritual law.

DREAMS COME TRUE

Ga Head Already

Deciding to take this big risk and move to Los Angeles was absolutely unforgettable. The way it all happened was so crazy. But I knew it was God.

I had planted my seeds in Los Angeles. I went to the Black Hollywood Film Fest, and I connected with my sister Gwen from the Unbroken Chain church who was now living in Los Angeles and bubbling. Lord God, is this what You want me to do?

Ga Head Already

Know that you know that you know.

Coincidence:
A situation in which events happen at the same time in a way that is not planned or expected.
- The occurrence of two or more things at the same time
- The state of two or more things being the same

Miracle

1 An extraordinary event manifesting divine intervention in human affairs.
2 An extremely outstanding or unusual event, thing, or accomplishment
3 Christian science: a divinely natural phenomenon experienced humanly as the fulfillment of spiritual law

The difference between coincidences and miracles is that miracles manifest divine intervention and fulfill spiritual law.

So, I was riding up Pennsylvania Avenue, and I made a left turn onto Atlantic Avenue. As I was entering onto the bridge, I prayed, "Lord, please, if You'd like for me to move to Los Angeles, please give me a sign." Just as I was finished praying at the middle of the bridge, my phone rang. I looked over to my phone. The area code was 310. I picked up, "Hello?"

"Hello, yes, is this Peter Moore?"

"Yes, it is. You recently submitted your picture for Charmed. Are you in Los Angeles?"

"No, I'm in Brooklyn."

"Okay, when can you be in LA? We'd like to see you for the television show Charmed." The light changed to green at the bottom of the bridge. I swung a right and pulled into the first parking spot. I had food on my lap. The food went everywhere. I jumped out of my car and started screaming, "Hallelujah, hallelujah, thank you, Jesus!" I was praising God in the street uninhibited. I jumped back in my car and started on my way back to my home. Drivers next to me noticed my excitement. They honked at me, "Share, share, why are you so happy?"

I hollered back, "I just got a call from a television show in LA!"

They shouted back, "Congratulations, all the best!" I pulled up to Warren Street and 4th Avenue in a huff. I had my marching orders. I was moving to LA.

Ga Head Already!

Know that you know that you know.

I got to the airport and collected my luggage. Gwen was right there, faithful as all out. Some of my luggage was missing. Gwen encouraged me that it would be there in the morning and that these kinds of things always happen. She had everything all planned out for me. At 5:00 am, I would rise with her. Start out my day at the 6:00 am prayer room at West Angeles Church. She said that this was the secret to her success in LA.

"6AM PRAYER AT WEST ANGELES CHURCH"

So, the morning came, and I went over to the prayer room. It was a small group. The room was full of wonder and awe. When the elder from the room came over to me, I felt like it was an old uncle who I hadn't seen in years. I felt connected to him immediately. Everyone quietly began to pray. Elder Taylor looked at me like, "Go ahead." This was so cool. Some were on their knees (most) on a little prayer mat. Others sat up. Some had prayer shawls. Some even paced up and down. Yet there was a synergy. Somehow there was a togetherness. Elder Taylor went to the mike and began to sing, "He's a wonder." We all came out of our personal prayer and joined in the song. Elder Taylor then led us into a small Bible reading, a mini sermon, prayer requests were prayed for, and we were out. Short and sweet.

Gwen and I then headed out to the airport, and yay, I got the rest of my luggage. I stayed some days with Gwen and her husband Anthony until my apartment at the Oakwood Apartments was ready. Gwen had referred me. When I walked into the Oakwood grounds, I just couldn't believe my eyes. I had no idea what to expect. I was really going to be actually living here. The pool was awesome. They had a gym and a computer room. My room was so, so cool, and in the distance in the mountains, I could see the Hollywood sign.

I had enough money to buy a car. I rented a car until the day finally came. That was a nightmare. There went most of my money. So, one day, I was driving on the 5 freeway way out into the mountains, lost. I exited to ask for directions back to Crenshaw Blvd. From there, I knew how to get anywhere (Thanks, Gwen!). So, I got off of the highway and drove past a used car lot, and there she was right in the middle of the lot, Bright Sparkly Red. I U-turned immediately. The guys in the small lot started laughing because they saw my reaction when I saw the car. They were Mexican cowboy Mustang gurus. They liked me right away. Long story short, I bought my first car for $5,000. I bought a classic 1966 hot red Ford Mustang. I named her Missy.

Black Beauty

Written Tuesday, September 22, 2015

I love wearing a tuxedo at the black and white affair. I love checking my bowtie for that special kind of flair. Catering in Los Angeles gave me the opportunity to have some of the most miraculous moments imaginable. Dressing up like Jimmy Hendrix and serving drinks and hors d'oeuvres at Donna Summers' birthday party with my new running buddy Angel Gaines was some of the best fun I've ever had while working ever. The party rooms were full of celebrities. Everyone was dressed up in their best black and white outfits. After a couple of drinks, heels were off, hookahs were out. Lounging and dancing and having a ball were all that it was all about. Yay, I was having a ball.

So, on this particular job, we went way out of the usual zone. Same tuxedo, black and white affair, yet this affair had a special touch. The grounds on this land were rich, and the dirt was red. Giant boulders (uncommonly large and beautiful, like quartz) lined the mountainside, and there were many personal gardens. It was really something to see. We had to set up a stage as well as tables and chairs on this expansive beautiful green lawn. The weather was perfect. We started to do our magic, and before you knew it, we transformed an open lawn into the most classy black and white luncheon affair you ever wanted to see. The grounds were run by a lot of Mexicans. The gardens were immaculate.

Well, well, well, of course, we were on the grounds of Mr. Dole's house, as in Dole pineapples, yessssssss. This special luncheon was for Mr. Dole's team. It was an appreciation celebration. Mr. Dole poured his heart out. He reiterated how special Dole was to him and how the Dole franchise was birthed. Mr. Dole was a health guru. So, he wanted to keep the world healthy. He created Dole foods.

While I was working, setting up for the event, Mr. Dole took the time to talk to me. He began to show me around the grounds. I asked him about the boulders lining the property and, of course, they had been shipped in. His hobby was raising Mustang horses. His horses were quietly in their stables. He promised me that he would bring some of them out to show me. I got so excited. The groundskeepers noticed and started cracking up. I had to stay focused on my job and not be distracted. But it was kind of noticeable. Mr. Dole had taken a liking to me. I was having a time with this very special, most beautiful person.

"Hey Peter, turn around!"

I turned around, and the whole world went into slow motion. I couldn't believe it. I backed up so that I could really get a good look. Yes, it was the most beautiful black horse that I had ever seen. He looked at me and whinnied. The crowd broke out in laughter. The handlers looked at me and said, "That means he likes you."

I was in total awe. I looked at this horse's muscular body and his strong neck and realized this was the most trained horse that I'd ever seen. You could tell that he was excited, but he wasn't moving. This horse stood there in one place and pranced like Mel Tomlinson at the Met. I said to Mr. Dole, "Wow, he's trained so well."

He said, "Of course. Do you know who you're looking at? This is Black Beauty. He has a SAG card just like you. He's not the first one. This is the first son. He has a family, but not all of them are black." Then the handlers brought out the mustang's wife and children. That's when the true nature of this Black Beauty showed his colors. He started snarling and getting agitated when anyone went too close to his wife and children.

Awesome. He was so powerful and could just run off and leave us all, but he didn't move in all of his passion. I'd always dreamed of seeing this horse and having this kind of experience. But I could have never imagined actually being with the actual horse that was in the movie.

Merry Christmas

I love it when you're just doing what you're supposed to do and God just showers you with all kinds of gifts. I was always happy to be working because I knew that I'd be having a check in a week or two. But some of my assignments gave rewards that could never be valued in dollars.

I liked working at the Malibu Beach Club only because I knew a good check was coming. The trip to Malibu from Long Beach was tricky. Night after night, I kept getting lost. One night on my way back from Malibu Beach, I missed my exit. The next exit was Compton. No way! You have got to be kidding me. I am in a shiny new '66 Mustang in a tuxedo lost, like really? Okay, here we go.

So, I got off in Compton, and I called my housemate. "Help, I'm in Compton. How do I get home?"

He said, "No worries, don't get back on the highway. I will guide you through the streets." As soon as I pulled off of the highway and read the sign "Welcome to Compton," there were a bunch of people out at a food stand. The whole stand looked over at me and started waving and calling at me. Ay yi yi, it was the car. I kept my head straight on and did not get out of the car to go to the food stand.

So now I was starting my way through these Compton streets. Wait, am I seeing correctly? No way, this can't be real. As I was going along the streets, I couldn't believe my eyes. The streets had the same exact names as East New York Brooklyn (where I grew up)—Milford, Essex, Bradford, and Blake. I couldn't believe it. I felt at home all of a sudden. All of the ignorant fear passed away, and before you know it, I was home.

John 14:16: And I will pray the Father, and he shall give you another Comforter, that he may abide with you forever.

Coincidence:
A situation in which events happen at the same time in a way that is not planned or expected.
- The occurrence of two or more things at the same time
- The state of two or more things being the same

Miracle
1 An extraordinary event manifesting divine intervention in human affairs.
2 An extremely outstanding or unusual event, thing, or accomplishment

3 Christian science: a divinely natural phenomenon experienced humanly as the fulfillment of spiritual law

The difference between coincidences and miracles is that miracles manifest divine intervention and fulfill spiritual law.

Malibu

Okay, so now that I had this Malibu, Long Beach trip down, here came the Malibu job that's on the other side of the Beach Club. Okay, so here we go. I finally got there. It was someone's home. These people had an annual Christmas party every year, and they hired a catering company for the party. The house was beautiful in a simple way. The maids who worked there began to show us around the kitchen. The maids were beautiful. The way that they cared for everything was as if they lived there. The maid quarters were off in the distance in the yard and were huge, like a nice-sized house in Queens. The living space was quaint, but the outdoor space was really nice. We built the tent and dressed the Christmas tables all out in the yard. Everyone stayed primarily in the dining space. The guests respected the home. The staff rotated. So sometimes I served in the dining area, and sometimes we served drinks in the house. I looked at the décor of the living room, and there were many pictures of the Kennedy's; interesting. These people must be in politics of some sort.

Wait a minute, really? Yes, really, you are at their home. Wait, is this Jacqueline Kennedy's home? OMG, no way. Yes way! I was at Jacqueline Kennedy's home. And yes, the Terminator himself was there.

OMG, it's Arnold Schwarzenegger's yearly Christmas party raising money for the disabled. Love it. Once the food was served and the guests had had a couple of drinks, it was pretty easygoing. Rob Reiner was the life of the party (I loved him in All in the Family). I was standing in the yard with a tray of drinks. I turned around, and there stood Arnold Schwarzenegger. I gasped for a moment. We were face to face. No way, I thought he was taller than that. He looked at me and rolled his eyes like, "Just pass me a drink, please." I handed him the drink and about-faced. Kenny G was sitting on a stool directly behind me. He was laughing. He said, "I saw that." He said, "That's okay, he's always uptight. This is a big night for him." For him, please, it was a big night for me as well! I had a blast. I was catering. But it was at one of the best annual Christmas parties ever. But damn, I couldn't make any connections. Chris Rock was trying to break me in. My heart was in my hands. But I had to stay professional. I heard him say to Macy Gray and crew, "I un know, something wrong, I un know." I couldn't be myself. I hated that moment. I wanted to chill and chat with Chris Rock and Macy Gray so bad. Anyways, Chris Rock finally figured it out and asked me to escort him into the backyard. That way, I would be still doing my job. I escorted Andre Harrell and Chris Rock into the backyard near the maid quarters for a cigarette break. Chris Rock was making sure that I heard the conversation and that I was close enough to catch a whiff. Man, I loved that moment so much. Me, Chris Rock, and Andre Harrell enjoying a smoke in Arnold Schwarzenegger's backyard...uuuugghhhh!

The party was ending, and the guests made their way out. Chris Rock and Macy Gray hung out in the quaint little room that I was tending to until the end. I didn't mind. I was enjoying every moment. When would I ever be at a Christmas party like this again?

Catering was definitely a good thing, but somehow, I didn't stay connected with the catering. I had come to Los Angeles to do acting, not catering.

Spirituals

So back to the lesson at hand, grinding, doing my thing thing in LA. I went to this audition for a Martin Luther King play. I got there, and I knew of the director from the New York dance world. I went in; he wanted me to reenact an innocent man being sprayed by a hose during the riots of the sixties. I did it. I had him. Then I had to sing. "Oh, nice, you have a great voice. Done! You're casted." Yay! I came to rehearsal, and the rest of the cast was older. Most of them were famous singers in gospel, R&B, and spirituals. As we moved along, the play morphed from a play about Martin Luther King into a spiritual musical review that most of the cast had done three times over. Now this was not what I had auditioned for. This was upsetting. I had come to act in this play. My strength in this here scenario was in my acting, not my singing. Especially not singing next to BeBe Winans! Ugh, I didn't come to LA for this. I left New York to come away from this type of show.

I loved this one particular part that I had because it showed off my acting. Well, it didn't hold up to the numbers that the cast knew and had performed many times over. The show was morphing into this showoff gospel review and that little blind harmonica player role that I had wasn't as important.

So, on this particular day, big dogs from the industry were coming to rehearsal to see what we had. My teacher from NCSA (North Carolina School of Arts) Mabel Robinson (The Wiz) was in the room. The director had me start my bit, then flippantly cut it out of the show. She watched my special role get ripped right out of my hands. My heart was ripped in two. That was my one moment to shine. Now I was just dancing and singing in the chorus. This was not what I had auditioned for. I had auditioned for an acting role. I did not audition for this project to be singing and dancing. Damn! Now I had been way pushed out in the scheme of the show. I had come to Los Angeles to do some acting. How did I end up in this gospel showcase singing and dancing review and now not acting at all? And I ain't even really getting paid. This was turning out to be a disaster. The director was now barking and snapping at me viciously because I was a little slow in getting the vocal material when the rest of the singers had already done this show three times over. I was done. This was it. I sat in rehearsal fuming; this was not what I had auditioned for. Please, I could just get in my car and drive away. OMG, and I was not getting paid. That's it. I'm just going to get in my car and drive away. I was just about to get up out of my seat and hop in my car and drive away. I looked around, and a cast member was pointing in my face. She said, "Don't you do it. I see you. God brought you here for a reason. Hold on. I see all that's happening with you." We had lunch together, and she calmed me down. We became rehearsal partners all the way through to the tech of the show. So, I was in my dressing room after the first tech, fuming still. I was still thinking about quitting. I didn't come to LA to be singing in this gospel arena. I came to act. I was in my dressing room fuming, getting undressed. I heard a knock on the door. I opened the door with my dance belt on.

It was Denzel Washington. I gasped and slammed the door in his face and then went crazy in my dressing room. I just slammed the door on Denzel. OMG, hold on, where's my clothes? I went spinning and turning in my dressing room. OMG, Denzel Washington! Finally when I got myself together and reopened the door, he was buckled over cracking up laughing. I started to apologize. He calmed me down, "No, no, no, it's okay." He shook my hand and said to me, "Everyone out there is going to remember the blind boy that you played."

I said, "Thank you, but the part that I had before it got cut and..."

He cut me off, "I know, I know, I know." While I was talking to him, my rehearsal partner was peeking out from behind Denzel Washington from side to side. I was looking at her like, "OMG, what are you doing? Stop it." Then the light bulb went off "Pling!" Oh wow, my rehearsal partner who got me through this whole process was Denzel Washington's wife. Hello, Pauletta Washington. Then we really cracked up because I had vented with her throughout the whole rehearsal process. That's why Denzel kept saying, "I know, I know." He really did know everything! Then we all really had a good laugh. I'm glad it happened that way because if I'd known that she was Denzel's wife, I wouldn't have been as genuine. My mind would have been preoccupied on asking her to meet him. It would have been all wrong. It was so great the way that that happened. After that tension had been broken, I was then honored to be in the project. It was so cool hanging around backstage with Denzel and his close church family circle for that time. Pauletta Washington really touched my heart for real.

I also really bonded with my mother in the play, Edna Wright (2/2/45-9/12/20 RIP). Who'd have guessed that I would have fallen so in love with the whole Perry family? They adopted me after this project. Edna Wright and I did have a very special part in Spirituals. She sang, and I did a "type nude" special modern dance as her dying son. It was hot. Her daughter Melody totally came to my rescue when the gospel boys were poking at my vocals. She whipped me in shape vocally as well as all others in the cast. I had a new sister friend. It was on.

Then years later, the coolest of the coolest happened. I actually opened the doors for Melody to get into the cast of the LA Lion King at the Pantages Theater. Yay! She got in. Now you know the family really loves me now, Blackatcha! We worshipped together, partied together, had each other's back, had good times and crazy times, and I met a real singing family. I wanted my Aunt May Fenty to meet Edna Wright, the singer of all of her favorite songs ("Want Ads," "Honey Cones"). Oh well, may they both rest in peace.

Back to the lesson at hand. Not only did I meet Denzel and his crew, but now I had a new family. This payment wasn't in dollars. It was in establishment and love. Man, did I end up really needing them. Things in Los Angeles started to get real rough. It was very hard to get a good workflow going.

(Turning the beat around...Love to hear percussion)

So, one day, I was visiting a friend who I met in the Black Hollywood Film Fest. He was shooting his film over by my new home in Long Beach, Cali. So, I got there, and lo and behold, who was there? Sonya Shepherd, my fellow cast swingmate from The Lion King. Sonya was in my buddy's film that actually won the Black Hollywood Film Festival favorite film award. It was hard letting Sonya know the real deal. But I couldn't believe that I was in LA and not working. She said, "Peter, I'm in the cast of Lion King here. Why don't you come backstage with me? You never know." So, I went with Sonya to the Pantages Theater. I got there, and they were having a major emergency. One of the swings mid-show caught a major injury, and there was no cover. No one would be on stage to work Timon's arm during the moon and stars scene with Simba. The LA cast's stage manager Lee was in a tizzy. Sonya introduced me to him. He said, "Wait a minute. You're the original cast swing from New York?"

I said, "Yes."

He said, "Then that means that Kale has your measurements?"

"Yes, I believe so."

He said, "If I threw you on stage right now, would you know what you're doing?"

I said, "Yeah." In my mind I said, "Of course, I set Timon's arms when we were creating it."

So, the company manager said, "Hey, you know what? I don't know what all went down with you guys in New York, but I have a show to run. Could you come in and go on tomorrow for me? I can start you with a two-week contract until we can figure things out. If he doesn't get better, I can keep you here with us, but when he gets better, I have to honor his contract and put him back in the show. Okay?"

"Okay!"

"So, welcome. Sonya, show him around."

Yay! Sonya, I love you.

Coincidence:
A situation in which events happen at the same time in a way that is not planned or expected.
- The occurrence of two or more things at the same time
- The state of two or more things being the same

Miracle
1 An extraordinary event manifesting divine intervention in human affairs.

2 An extremely outstanding or unusual event, thing, or accomplishment

3 Christian science: a divinely natural phenomenon experienced humanly as the fulfillment of spiritual law

The difference between coincidences and miracles is that miracles manifest divine intervention and fulfill spiritual law.

Tamarind Bar

Thank you, Sonya. Living in Long Beach was nice, but I couldn't rely on public transportation or lifts to get me to work when my car broke down. And my old girl (Missy, my '66 Mustang) was always in and out of the shop. Los Angeles had just put in their first underground subway. It was like a Coney Island, Great Adventures experience for the LA people. No one was seriously going to work. All of those folks were driving. I had to move closer to the theater.

The LA cast was so welcoming. I fell in love with them right away; everybody was willing to help. My car was old and troublesome, so I needed to be near the theater. Some of the coolest members of the cast had a spot near the theater and had a room open for me. I bunked in with them for a minute. And then, yay! One of the girls in the cast had decided to take a three-week vacation. She let me housesit her apartment while she was away. She was on Tamarind Lane. I love the street name. It reminded me of Barbados. At the corner of this very block (Tamarind Lane) was where all of the best LA fun happened. All of the cool stores and restaurants were right at my fingertips. The Bourgeois Pig was where all of the producers frequented. I was in the hippest part of town. The celebrity center was right across the street. I eventually ended up choreographing my friend Mary Randle's one-woman show Agape Love there. What a wonderful experience. I started to hang out night after night downstairs in my neighborhood, but I just wasn't vibing right. It didn't matter that I lived right up the block. I just was not gelling. I worked for a hot minute in the Hollywood souvenir store, and that was cool, but I still did not feel like I was in the fabric of the town. I started to drink more and more to bring down my inhibitions, thinking hopefully that I would make some strong connections here in LA. This led to some fun and crazy consequences but no real connections.

So, I was starting this new life in Los Angeles. Thank God for The Lion King. It really saved me and gave me a better run in Los Angeles. I still was all messed up. My car was down most of the time. My living situations were always temporary. The stage manager of the show (Lee) suggested that I move in with a cast member, Rock. Perfect, out of all of the cast members, he would be the one who I would want to roll with. I rolled with him for a little while.

Rock the Boat

I moved in with Rock on the Black Hollywood side. I also started attending Sonya's church in Inglewood. My journey quickly changed its colors.

The Los Angeles cast of The Lion King seemed to start poking and prodding at my living situation. The crazy subliminal and straight-out jarring messages, prodding and poking for me to try something that was not a part of my mind's equation. Things felt weird. Me and my new roommate's friendship was getting distorted. I began to distance myself from my roommate to let him know that I wasn't thinking about any kind of intimate relationship with him. Aw man. This was getting ugly. Every night after the show, my roommate went to his girlfriend's spot and either came back late or spent the night with her. I was cool with that. But I sure didn't want him to be scarce in his own home because of me. The pushing and the prodding and subliminal messages from the outside hyenas were irritating. I began to wonder. Wait a minute? Is this the reason that I moved here, to open up? My personal make-up was under attack. The vibes from the hyenas were gnawing at my soul. I really wanted to get along. Oh my God.

This is the real world. Let go and try something new. I wanted my roommate to be comfortable in his own home and have it the way that he wanted it. This was definitely a stumbling block on my journey of life. My roommate's welfare was now constantly on my mind. I began to think about all kinds of alternate life-style living situations. Okay, Peter, you're in Los Angeles. You're in Hollywood. This is part of it, play. My heart was torn. I surely did not come to Los Angeles for this. This was crazy. So, I finally got my things out of storage and settled in my now, new home with Rock for a while. This is it. Here we go. My stomach was unsettled. I unloaded my boxes and set up my new living space. I put up my two African statutes and looked around at my new reality. It was absolutely beautiful. Wow, here we go. Why does my stomach feel so unsettled?

Proverbs 10:22 states that the blessings of the Lord, it maketh rich and He addeth no sorrow to it. I was standing at the stop of the staircase. I prayed, "Father God, if this thing with my new roommate is something that You want me to go through, I'll do it, Lord God. But if You don't want me to live this kind of lifestyle, please let me know. I know that it's an adulterous nation that asks for a sign. But Lord God, please give me a sign, In Jesus's name, I pray." I opened my eyes, and immediately, an earthquake hit.

I started sliding down the staircase. The shaking stopped and left me wide-eyed and startled in the middle of the stair-case, clenching onto the rails. I looked across the way, through my neighbor's window, and my neighbor was in his home in the exact same position that I was in, on his staircase. He yelled out, "You okay?"

I said, "Yeah!" He started rambling on with instructions on what we needed to do if it hit again. Now mind you, this was the same neighbor who had bodyguards and entourages surrounding him in and out of his home every day. He could never speak to me because of his fame. He was speaking now. We sat still for a second; then we both came out of our homes and moved to the safest spot. Amazing how a crazy disaster can pull people together.

That earthquake's hit was not a coincidence. My heart was fixed. Right after I finished praying and asking God, Source, That for clarity, the earth shook. I now know that God did not want me to try some sort of crazy lifestyle that was not for me. I thank God that I came through it.

No Pain, No Gain

Coincidence:

A situation in which events happen at the same time in a way that is not planned or expected.

- The occurrence of two or more things at the same time
- The state of two or more things being the same

Miracle

1 An extraordinary event manifesting divine intervention in human affairs.

2 An extremely outstanding or unusual event, thing, or accomplishment

3 Christian science: a divinely natural phenomenon experienced humanly as the fulfillment of spiritual law

The difference between coincidences and miracles is that miracles manifest divine intervention and fulfill spiritual law.

Snoop Dogg

So, I got on the set of Snoop's "sha na na na nah" video, "Still Dre." It was a madhouse; everyone wanted to be in the video. They were calling the SAG (Screen Actors Guild) members first. Oh my goodness, when they called my name, the hatred started. I signed in and took my seat. Ignorant, overzealous, wannabe gang members were glaring at me. I just signed in, OMG. They were pointing, "Him, him." Changing seats in front of me. Walking away and then coming back with someone else staring and pointing at me trying to get me to react. A lot of the people on this set were actually gang members, so this was really getting crazy. Out of the blue, one of my sisters from the Unbroken Chain in New York who used to give me a lift from time to time to the Bronx was on set. Yay! Centria! She looked so beautiful and gorgeous. She knew the guys who were doing the musical chairs in front of me. She was connected in the gang-life in LA. Of course, she's ride-or-die like that. When she saw me, she ran over to me. She did it to let them know, "This is my friend from New York. No! Leave him." She told me not to tell anybody in NY that she was in Los Angeles and doing this video. I was like, "Centria, please, do your thing, we both out here." The shoot was crazy. Niggas was going buck wild. The girls didn't want to be touched the way they were being touched. Snoop came out and was like, "Yo! Listen up, this is what it is. If you can't hang, get off the set." I looked over at Centria, and a male porn star (Jake Steed) was standing directly behind Centria, about to coax her into a back room that was off set. She looked at me. We gave each other that look, and she pulled out. She snuck off set early before things got too rough. I stayed. Then the fire really turned up. Snoop walked over to me. He liked my getup. He said, "Yo, New York (my now-new video name), when honey comes down this pole, I want you to take this dollar in your hand and slap it right there, slap. The same Spanish girl who was talking mess about she don't want to be touched and whoever is at the bottom of the pole when she comes down is going to get her heels in their face. Yes, you, open your legs. Look, New York, slap, just like that." Oh man, now that Snoop gave me that special direction, you know everybody was jealous of me now. I was being crowded all around because everyone wanted to be in the shot. This one very odd London-accented, all leather character befriended me, and then a girl. When it was time to leave, I just felt like, "Oh my God, it's over. "The parking lot was wilding out at the end of the shoot. We were in a bad area in downtown Los Angeles. Damn, and Missy (my car) was looking splinkity. My new London friend told me that him and some friends were going clubbing after the shoot and asked if I wanted to come. So, I said okay. Turns out that he didn't have a ride off set. Cool, so now I had a girl and this crazy-looking, leathered-out, fake London-accented guy to drive off of the set with, shwheew! Made it, sha na na na nah, that was a crazy, tripped-out adventure.

Maybe about a month later, I was driving down Crenshaw Blvd. on my usual trip back home from work. I noticed some very cultured-looking black girls standing on the corner. Wait a minute, slow down. This was definitely a rare sight. They looked like Brooklyn girls. They had flava. Eerks, U-turn, what is this? All condensed in one area. This must be the opening of some new club or something. I'd never seen this before. So, I pulled into the parking lot, parked, and then made my way over to the entrance. The girl at the door was very nice, smiley, and welcoming.

I looked at her bewildered like, "Hi. Where in the world did all of these girls with flava come from? This is so rare here in Los Angeles. Wow, this is nice." I made my way over to the bar and sat in amazement at the beauty all around me. Then it dawned on me. Hmm, where are the men? I must be early or something.

Folks don't know about this spot yet. Hmm, still no guys. Then I heard this girl going off on this other girl behind a wall. The girl who was yelling was getting angrier and angrier. It was if she was letting the other girl know that "You're about to get your ass beat!" I was enjoying my drink. I always try to stay out of other people's business. But another girl came around the bend, and it seemed like they were both getting ready to rip into this girl. But they made sure she was behind the wall so that no one could see. So, I decided to get up and leave this scene. When I stood up, I decided to take a look at this girl who was about to get beat up.

And lo and behold, guess who it was? It was Centria. I screamed out, "Centria!" She looked over at me. Ran over to me and fell in my arms. The girl who was yelling at her immediately came over to interject. I put up my hand and stopped her. Hold on. The girl was still ready to give orders. Hold on, hold on. I shut her up. I pulled Centria away. "Centria, are you okay?"

She looked me in my eyes in disbelief. "OMG, Peter, Peter, over here." I looked back at the girl like, "Back up, I got this." Centria moved me a little further away from her terrorizer. "Peter, OMG, what are you doing in here?"

"Walk with me over here." I told her I had just fallen on this place and that I lived nearby and had my car in the back, if she needed to leave, what? We moved to another part of the bar. Her terrorizers were close behind. Then Centria found her crew.

"Oh yes, thank you, Peter, I'm good now." She unlocked arms with me and ran over to her crew. Her friends called her.

"Centria, where were you?" She joined her pack of girls, and she was herself again. She came back over to me

"Peter, thank you, thank you. You have no idea what you just did. But, you can't stay here. This is an all-girls night out. These girls are going to act out on you if you stick around any longer."

"Okay, Centria, are you really okay? I know my way around Los Angeles now. Plus, I have my Thomas guide on me. We could leave right now if you want to."

"No, I'm good, but you, you better get out of here."

"Okay, I'm going to leave, be good, love you, sister."

"Love you too, my brother." I pulled off onto Crenshaw Blvd and continued on my trip home.

Okay, now come on. How crazy was that? Centria saved me on the set of Snoop's "Still Dre" video, wow, and I ended up saving her at this round the way party. Was it a coincidence that I decided to take the streets instead of getting on the 10 highway? Was it a coincidence that I decided to go straight home instead of staying on Hollywood Blvd and having a social drink there? Was it a coincidence that I decided to sit and have my drink directly across from where Centria's terrorizer was about to beat her up?

Coincidence:
A situation in which events happen at the same time in a way that is not planned or expected.
- The occurrence of two or more things at the same time
- The state of two or more things being the same

Miracle
An extraordinary event manifesting divine intervention in human affairs.

- An extremely outstanding or unusual event, thing, or accomplishment
- Christian science: a divinely natural phenomenon experienced humanly as the fulfillment of spiritual law

- **The difference between coincidences and miracles is that miracles manifest divine intervention and fulfill spiritual law.**

The difference between coincidences and miracles is that miracles manifest divine intervention and fulfill spiritual law.

I Need Help

No Pain, No Gain

It's one of the craziest things of our existence. Why would an all-knowing and loving God manifest Himself on earth and then kill Himself?

Why does prejudice exist?

Why are some people sexually attracted to children?

Why this, why that. Why, why, why. Who knows why?

I really had bonded with my brothers at The Faithful Central Church in Inglewood. They had my heart. I loved the study and prayer circles that I had with them. But outside of church, I couldn't really roll with them. The brother who I had bonded with the most headed the prayer group that I was in. He rolled his sleeves up and really tried to be a great brother. When I felt all disheveled and pushed out, he moved me in with his brother near him and his family. His brother and I bonded immediately. My buddy owned a barber shop. I started getting my hair cut there. Some of the brothers from the prayer group were there. I loved going there and getting my hair cut. But I still wasn't really rolling with them. I was still broke, and these guys were balling.

And...I really couldn't find a love for me. It was noticeable. I was always alone. That is a red flag for most guys and most of the other churches that I joined along my journey. That same red flag rose up. Painful. So, it felt like I was really at the end of my rope. I really couldn't believe that I had to move again. I had very little money. I asked all of the guys from the prayer group for help. Only one of them could come through. Of course, Anthony, the leader. And he couldn't stay for long. What in the world was I going to do? I prayed, and in anger, I wrote in bold capital letters on a piece of nearby scrap paper, "I NEED HELP." Painful!

I continued to pack my things up. I drove over to the U-Haul spot. As I was approaching the entrance, I saw all of these Mexicans jumping up and waving. What were they waving at? As I got closer, it looked as if they were waving at me. They were, and they were yelling out, "You need help, you need help? Me and my friend, we do good work, ten dollars."

"Ten dollars for the both of you?"

"No, ten dollars each, Papi."

"Oh, okay, okay, wow." OMG, thank you, thank you, thank you for that.

Answered prayer :)

I was feeling so broken and hurt because only one of my brothers showed up for me, and then he left. Those two Mexican guys moved me so well. They were so cheap. I was able to buy a pizza and a bottle of Sprite for them. They were so happy, and I made my move.

Move past the pain and move on.

Yucca

Moving on Yucca Street was so exciting. Jennifer was from Africa. She was the perfect roommate. I was now living right off of Hollywood Blvd again. I loved it. And right across the street from the Pantages Theater where The Lion King was playing. I would only go in if they had a real emergency because the cast was pretty tight with their swings and backups. Wow. Imagine that, I was the original cast swing of this Broadway musical, and now I was living across the street from where it was playing. Unemployed. Really? Talk about painful. Well, it was what it was.

Yucca!

I thought Jennifer was going to be the perfect roommate. She was African. She always brought her cooked lunch with her back-stage. I thought that she had cooked. I assumed that she cooked. Eeeersk. Wrong, she ordered out. Also, when she showed me the apartment, it was so sweetly furnished and warm. When I moved in, Jenifer moved out all of the furniture. Damn. I didn't have money to buy furniture. Okay. I put my computer and some of my things in my new room and left to get the rest of my things. When I came back, my new laptop was gone. The only two people in the apartment were Jennifer and her boyfriend. Ugh. Now I had trust issues. Jennifer broke up with that guy but soon got another boyfriend, who liked to sit his shoes outside of her bedroom door.

The smell was so strong that even with my doors closed, I could smell his stink feet. Yucca.

But whenever I wanted to hang out, I could just get dressed and just walk right outside my door onto Hollywood Blvd. I loved it. Jennifer and I made it work. But we weren't really gelling. Tensions started to grow. When The Lion King's run came to an end, Jennifer didn't want to go home. Going back to Africa was torment for her. She was making such good money with The Lion King, and now she had to go home to nothing. I loved Jennifer's talent. I told her that she should try to make money in LA. It wouldn't work. LA was too rough for her. She couldn't get all drugged out. She always had an eye for me. I loved her like a sister. But I had no sexual attraction to her. This became a problem I was being forced to engage. Because if I married Jennifer, she could stay here in the US and make money. Ugh. The tension was all around. I hated it. I was having enough problems trying to keep good-paying survival jobs and still pursue my performing career. Man.

And then I got jumped.

No pain, No gain

This night was where it all went haywire. I was filling in part-time for the show on a day-to-day and week-to-week contract and living right across the street. This was really throwing me off, all the last-minute calls. So, on this particular night, I woke up around 7:25, ran across the street and signed in, half a warm-up, and bam, I hurt my ankle doing the hyena dance. Instead of reporting it, I continued. I was there to save the show, not to be another casualty.

So, now I was limping, uh oh. I was really hurt. The performance was a special performance, and the cast was going to celebrate on the Blvd. I didn't feel like hanging out with the rest of the cast. I really didn't have that kind of camaraderie with any of the cast members. Plus, I was limping. So, I went around the back of the theater to be away from them. I wanted to get a drink, but I didn't want them to see where I was going. So, I decided to go up behind the Pantages Theater into Hollywood Hills and venture on the backside of the Blvd to get to the other side (limping). Long story short, I got into a scuffle with three guys.

FIGHT!

I really hurt the main offender by kicking him in the balls. He was laid out on the floor. I went to go on top of him, and his buddy grabbed my collar. As I moved toward the guy on the ground, my jacket and shirt ripped off. The guy on the floor reached for his gun in his right pocket. The guy standing said, "Wait, don't shoot him!" When I saw the gun, I got off of the guy on the floor and jumped down a flight of stairs and headed for the bottom of the building. I heard them arguing behind me. I kept running. Finally, I got to the bottom of the stairs. I got onto Hollywood Blvd. I was out of breath. When I got to the Blvd, everyone was looking at me and smiling. They thought it was some sort of Hollywood Blvd entertainment thing. I was a little bloody. The tourists thought this was a Blvd spectacle. So, I ran into the street to cause commotion. In LA, jaywalking is not accepted. Finally, a cab pulled up. I asked him to please pull off because I only lived just up the block, and I didn't want the guys who'd attacked me to see where I lived. He let me in the cab. I looked at my thumb, and it was loosely swinging about. I couldn't even feel it. When the cab dropped me off at Yucca, I went through the gate and tried making it over to my apartment door. That's when it really hit me. I couldn't walk over to my door. I limped myself over to my door and then got inside and called the stage manager from Lion King and told him what had happened. The rest was history. Hobbling along, still trying to maintain my rent with a roommate who was upset and threatened that the show was closing.

Ooh wee, we had some trying good days.

Although I was living on Hollywood Blvd, the struggle to come into the life that I wanted to live was extremely hard. So, I guess this is what brought out the super spiritual side of me. I was living on Hollywood Blvd, but I wasn't making sufficient income to enjoy the fun of it. It was no fun going to a great club and not being able to buy drinks or even treat someone to a drink. I would wake up every morning and go past Paramount onto Wilshire Blvd, where I fantasized of living, and then onto Crenshaw Blvd over into the prayer room. They were my saving grace. I came to love it, and especially, Elder Taylor. It was magnificent to see how God used him to change people's lives daily. So, although I was in the center of Sin City, I found my joy back in Crenshaw at West Angeles Church's prayer room. Jennifer was in and out and back and forth for long periods of time. So, I spent most of my time on Yucca Street by myself.

Oscars

One day, I was in my apartment alone with no cable and internet, half living, feeling horrible about the experience that I had had the night before. I looked on the TV, and they were having great big preparations on Hollywood Blvd for the grand opening of the Kodak Theater. I was watching this whole event on TV thinking, Wow, this looks wonderful. But then it dawned on me. How are they filming that the way that they are? If they are taping shots like that, that must mean that my block is blocked off, and I'm inside of the event. So, this must mean that if I step outside of my doors, I will, by default, be at the Oscars. I took my disheveled self out of my front door and noticed no traffic. I walked to the corner, and sure enough, the event was in full effect. I was at the grand opening of the Kodak Theater by default. I had an open invitation to the Oscars because I lived here on Yucca. So cool.

I met some rodeo guys and a black cowboy, and they bought me drinks all night as we enjoyed the celebration.

Wow, what a night. Sigh.

Okay, back to my lonely apartment on Yucca. Jennifer was in and out in her preparation to make her trip back home to Africa. I guess the neighbors considered me snotty or something because they began to ridicule me as I went to and fro daily. They thought that Jennifer was my girl and she was leaving me, so they were laughing at me in this critical time. I couldn't pay the rent on Yucca alone. So, once again, I had to move. I made a special agreement with the Oakwood Apartments. I couldn't afford to stay there for the whole while, but a couple of months could hold me over until I got another apartment that I could really settle into. This whole ordeal was so irritating. But I knew that somehow, I would be okay.

The day finally came, and I had to be out of the apartment by a certain hour. I couldn't afford a truck. The cost of moving back into the Oakwood Apartment had taken all of my money. I didn't have much. If I did it right and drove real slow, I believed that everything could fit inside of my Mustang. So, I started to pack her up as methodically as I could. And then it started to rain. My neighbors went under their car sheds, popped some beers, and enjoyed the show. As I rushed to get my car packed, as the cardboard boxes started to break because of the rain, as Jennifer passed back through to check if she had left anything with a mad and upset spirit, they were cracking up and laughing and drinking and enjoying the show. I was soaked now and struggling to get all of my things loaded into the car. The rainstorm was unusual. Los Angeles doesn't have storms like this all of the time. It was kind of eerie. There were ravens circling above my car. There was obviously something dead on the roof. The sky was cloudy and silent; lightning flashes were lighting up the sky.

Finally, I was all packed up. Here we go. I pressed the remote for the gate, and the gate wouldn't open. My neighbors fell out laughing. It was an electrical storm. It had knocked out the power of the gate. OMG. How was I going to get out? I pressed the remote again. The gate didn't open. My neighbors fell out laughing and pointing at me with tears in their eyes. Hilarious. I kept pressing the remote for the gate to open. Now what was I going to do? I dropped my head in despair and prayed. I could hear the laughter as I was praying. When I lifted my head and opened my eyes, we all heard a loud buzz, and the gate began to slide back. My audience applauded and waved at me as I slowly pulled out of the gate.

- Yucca Street electrical storm, gate opener

Focus

Pop, pop, pop! Uh oh, gunshots. Pop, pop! Uh oh, someone's shooting back. Pop, pop! Woah, hello, that was too close. What in the hell? Did somebody just run past my window? Ugh, stay down. Is that someone on the front porch? Oh, no. Aw man, he is running right next to my window. Noooo! He's running and hiding in our yard. Oh no! Pop! Oh, shit, pop, pop, shots in the backyard. That's the gate; they climbed over the gate.

Blamm! My bedroom door slammed open.

"Peter!"

"Yes?"

"You okay?"

"Uh, yes."

My roommate was mad as hell with two huge guns in his hands. "These motherfuckers don't understand. My Mother left me this house. I don't play that shit. You don't come through this yard with that bullshit. These Motherfuckers should know better." My roommate then about-faced with his pajamas on and his loaded gun and headed toward the backyard. Slam, the backyard door opened. He paced up and down and scoped the yard out. "Hell, no!" waving his gun. "They should know way better than to come up and through this yard with that bullshit. People got to go to work. I don't play that."

I sighed and just stayed laying in my bed like, "What in the world just happened?" as my roommate began to prepare to leave for work. My mind was trying to put a wrap on what was really happening here. Finally, he was dressed and leaving for work. "Yo, Peter, you don't have anything to worry about here, okay? If you hear them mother@#$%'s round here with that bullshit again, you call me. I got something for they asses."

"Okay, thanks. Have a good day at work."

"Aight, and you be aight, okay? Just call me if you need anything..."

"Okay." I laid down quietly for a moment. Then fear was trying to settle in with crazy imaginations. I was not rising above the windows, nor was I moving out of the room. OMG. Really, did that just really happen? That was worse than when the Tomahawks and the Sex Boys had their gang war right in front of our house at 282 Montauk Avenue in East New York Brooklyn when I was a child. I was out here in Los Angeles alone. This was not good. My mind started to imagine all sorts of things. Like what if my roommate had set that up? What if all of that was just to scare me? I didn't want to be played with like that. Why would they come through this yard? I shouldn't be sleeping in this front room. These walls are thin. Okay, get up. Don't let fear set in. Open the door and go sit in the yard. They won't come this way if they know that someone is at home.

So, I got out of the bed, grabbed my Bible, and decided to go into the yard and pray. I went and sat under his gazebo in the yard. The day was beautiful. The smells in the yard were amazing. I looked up, and the gazebo was covered in little tangerines. The flowers were in full bloom, rare and beautiful. I closed my eyes and took in the amazing smells all around me. I could hear some fighting not too far away still going on. I felt the warmth of the sun shining directly on me, and when the wind blew, I could smell the sweet smells of the fruit and the flowers in the yard. The fussing and fighting became softer. I kept my eyes closed, and I started to pray. The smells and the warm air moved my soul into this sweet, sweet place of enlightenment. Just then, I heard the fence move. I kept my eyes closed. The sounds of footsteps got closer and closer and then stopped. I could almost see through my eyes the person standing on the outside of the gate staring at me. I went deeper into prayer. I let go and entered into one of the bravest in-synced moments with God, Source, That of my life.

Just then, in my inner ear, I heard, "Focus." I continued to bask in the synchronicity, and then I heard, "Focus." The warmth of the sun and the smells of sugar cane, olives, and tangerines in the yard made me forget all about where I was and how the morning had actually started out.

I heard, "Focus." I was settled, calm, and at peace. "Focus." I slowly opened my eyes, and a hummingbird was beak to nose with me, forehead to forehead. My right eye laser-focused right into the hummingbird's left eye. We agreed on it. While we were eye to eye, there was a slight blur behind his eye. That was the bird's wings flapping so fast that my natural eye couldn't even see it. In the flash of a second, we broke focus, and the hummingbird flew away. The bird flew away, but the interaction we had will never fade away. I received a miracle message that day from the hummingbird.

22And he said unto his disciples, Therefore I say unto you, Take no thought for your life, what ye shall eat; neither for the body, what ye shall put on. 23The life is more than meat, and the body [is more] than raiment. 24 Consider the ravens: for they neither sow nor reap; which neither have storehouse nor barn; and God feedeth them: how much more are ye better than the fowls? 25And which of you with taking thought can add to his stature one cubit? 26If ye then be not able to do that thing which is least, why take ye thought for the rest?

Vuyo's But Theory

BUT God changed his mind
Law killeth
BUT the Spirit giveth life
But I am a sovereign God
But our ways are not his ways
But you survived

Whenever you see the BUT,
Just know,
Despite all of our shortcomings, miracles will still happen.

You could have spent your time reading someone else's book. BUT instead, you decided to read this book, and while reading it, you received divine revelation that was so personal to you that the interaction let you know, this had to be God.

Peter Anthony Moore

ABOUT THE AUTHOR

———————◆———————

Peter Anthony Moore was born in Brownsville, Brooklyn, New York. Peter graduated from the New York High School of Performing Arts as sole recipient of the Playbill Award. Dancing with Alvin Ailey started his professional performing career. Dancing with Alvin Ailey has afforded Peter the honor of dancing on most of the New York stages including Carnegie Hall and The Met. Peter assisted Alvin Ailey in creating the ballets Magica Caverna and Inside. He later went on to assist George Faison in the choreographing "Mad pain" for the opening celebrations of the 1996 Olympic games. The musical A Chorus Line taught Peter to sing. He made his Broadway debut when he became an original cast member of Disney's The Lion King. Peter became a Screen Actors Guild member and has been seen in many New York film and television productions, such as "I Love NY" commercial, When in Rome, Thanks for Sharing, Ugly Betty, Confessions of a Shopaholic, and many more. Peter is presently focusing on his multimedia artwork and striving to make "Mbewu" a world-changing brand.

CPSIA information can be obtained
at www.ICGtesting.com
Printed in the USA
LVHW071631280322
714614LV00018B/986

9 781662 842153